UNDERDOG

UNDERDOG

12 INSPIRATIONAL STORIES
FOR THE DESPONDENT
LAW STUDENT

JESSE WANG

NEW DEGREE PRESS

COPYRIGHT © 2020 JESSE WANG

All rights reserved.

UNDERDOG

12 Inspirational Stories for the Despondent Law Student

ISBN   978-1-63676-568-6   *Paperback*

    978-1-63676-160-2   *Kindle Ebook*

    978-1-63676-161-9   *Ebook*

I would like to dedicate this book to my sister, Lisa, who has constantly inspired me to be independent and to keep pushing forward no matter how many times I fall. To my dear friends Crystal, Jessica, Marissa, Owen, Cathy, James, and Gabby who have helped me through some of the more difficult moments I experienced during my time as an undergraduate and as a law student. I would also like to thank my parents for the opportunities they've afforded me throughout the years. I am grateful that they allowed me to gain a quality education at The Shipley School, Emory University, and the University of Southern California.

This book is also dedicated to the USC Barbara F. Bice Public Interest Law Foundation (PILF). Founded in 1988, PILF is a student-run, nonprofit organization that promotes social justice lawyering, equal access to the law, and the empowerment of marginalized and underrepresented communities by providing pro bono clinic opportunities at local organizations, hosting lectures on key issues, and supporting students in public interest work over the summer through a grant program.

Profits from Underdog book sales will go toward funding law students pursuing public interest work, as well as other pro bono clinic opportunities.

CONTENTS

———

Success is the ability to go from one failure to another with no loss of enthusiasm.

—WINSTON CHURCHILL

ACKNOWLEDGMENTS

I'd like to acknowledge those who have given this book, and the stories within it, legs strong enough to move forward:

Gilbert Bradshaw, Julie Svigals, Chanel DuPree, Ricca Prasad, Pablo Aabir Das, Janet Boachie, Susan Booth, Donald Li, Yvette Lopez, Carlos Ochoa, Catherine Pan, Hongyan Li, Dez Leon, James Lewis, Jason Ridgill, Mark Gannott, Julia Spathis, Gurbani Singh, Nicolette Karanfilian, Jalyn Radziminski, Joseph Egbule, Reena Patel, Kathleen Radich, Jingru Zhao, Kevin Doran, Jennifer Wilson, Katie Hill, Sanjay Velappan, Clare Garvie, Nicole Okafor, Helena Sermak-Proulx, Amanda Henry, Emile Nelson, Trinh N Truong, Kathleen M Lee, Alisha Nguyen, Ann Majchrzak, Dami Kim, Shama Hassan, Michael Larson, Tracey Laboz, Emily Bratt, Marc E. Empey, Laura Hilado, Connie Wang, Rafael Tavarez, Ida Ayu, Sabrina Putri, Mindy Amornwichet, Diana Stephanie Lara, Mindy Vo, Kayla Blaker, Paul Caintic, Akiko Okamoto, Ben Goldfein, Ellie Goldman, Will Mavity, Mirandy Li, Olivia M. Treister, Charlene Smith, Anissa Ghafarian, Herinda Castagnoli, Char Weigel, Marisa DiGiuseppe, Beah Tolentino, Ananya Anmangandla, Mira Pranav, Shams

Sohani, Owen Ticer, Krisha Cabrera, Michael Roster, Jonathan Chen, Samantha Delbick, Kathryn Pacheco, Lisa Wang, Zach Shen, Kevin Coyle, Chelsea Landman, Olivia Odle, Max Kohl, Emily Rohles, Michael Chasalow, Kayla Fallick, Michael Keen, Bellee Jones-Pierce, Jonathan Chen, Lina Zhang, Lauren Rhea, Brian Raphael, Samantha Dyar, Gabrielle Rodrigues, Diana Lam, Danielle Marhanka, Krystal Robles, Erin Oquindo, Aminah I, Ian Wood, Brooke Mulligan, Ravneet Purewal, Tatum Rosenfeld, Sonia Ghura, Alicia Lu, Alina Edep, Rebecca Brown, Forest Lieberman, James Reizman, Mirelle Raza, Sue Wright, Sonal Imbulamure, Anastasio Sapalidis, Marty Noel Chenyao, Justina Huang, Ebony Love, Victor Chatman, Marissa Pham, Courtney Mendoza, Nicholas Connolly, Kiran Sundar, Ken Rodriguez, Jonathan Hechler, Emma Arroyo, Javid Kazimi, Yinan Kang, Reshma Shah, Crystal Tan, Juliette Browne, Aigerim Saudabayeva, Hanna Laikin, Luke Bickel, Diana Chen, Alvincé Pongo, Katherine Evans, Claire Reidy, Rebekah Baird, Eric Koester, Carlos Ochoa, Scott H Bice, Matteo Jin, Rebecca Li, Kelly Luo, Jessica Lin, Angela Hwang, Christine Kades, Chris Bostrom, Shih-Yu Wu (Claire), Tyler Scott, Xunxie Wang, Danielle Luchetta, Sophia Ye Fang, Kristin Bradley, Sonia Shen, Allison Skager, Amy Lutfi, Dorna Moini, Joie Wu, Amanda Tran, Pitrina Gilger, Ashley Smith, Owen Lynch, Alaina Ross, Julia Abovich, Eleanor Hazard, Taha Rizvi.

Lastly, I'd like to acknowledge a few sources of inspiration:

Angela Lee Duckworth, Andrew Yang, Amy Chua, Mariah Carey, Jordan Peterson, Nassim Nicholas Taleb, Gabriel García Márquez, Issa Rae, Wong Kar-wai and Ocean Vuong.

AUTHOR'S NOTE

———

"Can you explain to me...these grades?" the recruiter asked smugly, as he looked up from the transcript in his hand. I stared back hollowly. My eyes felt tired. I didn't even have to look in the mirror; I could feel the dark circles becoming increasingly pronounced as the day dragged on. Part of me wanted nothing but to wipe that smug look off his face. I wanted to flip the table over, storm out of the room, and flip everyone off on my way out. But I held back because he wasn't the problem. He was just a symptom of it.

Normally, if I were in a stressful situation, I'd sweat profusely and talk at a breakneck pace. But I wasn't stressed at all. I had no expectation of getting any callbacks that day. In fact, my hopes of getting an offer from one of the dozens of firms I had signed up to interview with were extinguished long before on-campus recruiting had even begun. It was my eighth interview of the day, and I felt dead inside. I smiled meekly. "It's a long story. Maybe I'll write about it someday," I said as I chuckled to myself.

There are two instances I remember most vividly from my first year of law school. The first was when I got my fall semester grades back, and the second was when I got my spring semester grades back. Everything else was a blur. And I am thankful for that because the first year of law school is without a doubt the most stressful experience of my life thus far.

The entire summer after my first year, I felt like I was in a state of purgatory. I was working at a pro bono immigration clinic in East Los Angeles—the Los Angeles Center for Law and Justice, or LACLJ for short. It was a ninety-minute commute each way. I had to take the metro from USC to 37th Street, hop on the Metro Silver Line to get to Grand, switch to the 720 shuttle to get to Whittier, and then, to top it all off, I had to walk a mile to finally get to the office. Long commutes tend to make me feel lonely and depressed, and so I tried my best to keep my mind occupied with podcasts like *This American Life*, *NPR Life Kit*, and *Help Me Be Me* by Sarah May B. But when Ira Glass and Shankar Vedantam's voices couldn't distract me anymore, my anxiety crept in.

I remember staring out the window of the Metro with my headphones on, conjuring up fake scenarios of how OCI would go. How would I present myself? What would I say? How could I avoid having to run out of the room in tears when the recruiter laughs in my face when they see my transcript? Those long commutes were hot, exhausting, and filled with rumination. My mind's ability to fixate and dwell on iotas of past memories was astonishing.

I thought about what I could've done differently. What if the grades I got were because I didn't go to office hours that one time because I was sick? What if they were because I didn't do enough practice tests? Or because I blinked and missed half a fragment of my property professor's irrelevant meanderings about his pomelo tree? None of it mattered anymore. But somehow all of it still mattered to me. At least in my head.

When the summer finally came to a close, OCI immediately began to ramp up into overdrive. Just when we were all burnt and ironed out from the slaughter-fest that was our first year of law school (commonly known as "1L" or sometimes "1Hell") and our summer jobs, it was time to chug full steam ahead into the devil's snare—the USC Hotel, the place where law firms from all over the country would come to set up shop and court law students to be part of their summer associate programs.

I signed up for almost two dozen interview slots through the bidding system and landed about ten initial interviews. I thought to myself: People literally dream about OCI for years before going into law school. The bruised and beaten optimist in me shouted from the bottomless pit he had fallen into, *"Just give it a go! Why the hell not?"*

OCI was about a week long for me. On the first day, I entered through the front door with a smile plastered on my face with gorilla glue. I went through the motions and kept my tone bright and posture straight during all my interviews. And with gritted teeth and a dampened spirit, I came out of the hotel without a single callback. I felt like a factory reject. I was defective. They didn't want me. I didn't belong.

Looking back on OCI and my first year in law school, I can still see exactly how and why I felt the way that I did. I think we often hear stories about why people want to attend law school that are somewhere along the lines of "I want to change the world" or "I want to help people." But, miraculously, this community-oriented sentiment disappears as soon as people hear about how much lawyers make at big law firms (or "big law" for short). In the snap of a finger, getting into big law becomes everything for many such individuals.

Granted, there's nothing wrong with striving to make more money, especially when you're drowning in student debt. At that point, big law almost becomes necessary. But there are also many people who aren't as economically deficient, yet still break their backs to receive promotions, to earn larger incomes, or to get ahead in life in some other status-driven way. I'm not going to lie, that stuff's important to me too. But after everything I've learned from my first year of law school, I would never make it my number one priority.

I admit, I was certainly blinded for a long time by the splendor and grandeur of it all. It was like I was conditioned within the first month of entering law school to put getting a 4.0 GPA at the top of my bucket list, one rung above living a fulfilling life, forming meaningful relationships, and creating a better society for myself and for those around me. But, of course, this was all before I learned how law school classes were structured.

When people said law school (or graduate school in general) was like drinking water out of a fire hydrant with a straw, they were lying. It's not like that at all. It's like drinking water from Kaieteur Falls. Except instead of a straw, you get a coffee stirrer. And instead of water, it's actually a cocktail of self-hatred, depression, nihilism, anxiety, and vodka.

Basically, for every class, you have to read anywhere between six and twelve incredibly dense cases, each of which has perhaps half a sentence that contains the actual law that may be somewhat relevant on the final exam, which, by the way, is worth 100% of your entire semester grade. Oh, and the exam is a timed issue spotter, where you're given a hypothetical scenario and you have to spot and apply every single legal principle you learned throughout the entire semester, type it out, and submit it within 2.5 hours. In summary: Your ability to get an offer at a prestigious law firm, your status among your peers, and the entirety of your self-worth depends on how you perform on that exam.

My self-esteem going into law school looked like a Greek god with winged slippers and a silk chiton woven by a seamstress from Ming dynasty China. And coming out of OCI, it looked like someone had thrown it under a lawnmower, sprayed it with gasoline, lit it on fire, and extinguished it using sludge from the Great Pacific Garbage Patch.

I honestly have no clue why I didn't just drop out and go home. I think that broken and battered optimist in me just wouldn't die. I've always had this inner spark that just keeps echoing within the inner spiral cavity of my ear: "What if... suddenly things get better? What if this isn't the end? What if you just kept going?" I mean, I had gotten through the worst year of my life, and I was still standing. Why not just give my second year a fighting chance?

Staying another year was a difficult decision, but it's one that I do not regret at all. Throughout my second year of law school, I met so many incredible people, including lawyers, classmates, and entrepreneurs, who completely changed my perspective on academics and success in life. Each of them taught me an important lesson, with the central message that success isn't about short-term results or how you perform on an issue-spotting exam. Instead, they showed me that success is about appreciating small wins and using them to build momentum to achieve bigger wins in the future. Success is about building a network of people with similar mindsets like yours and who can support you in the face of adversity. Most importantly, success is about resilience—persevering day in and day out and chasing down a singular goal with every ounce of your being.

I want to say I wrote this book so that every time a recruiter or a partner asks me, "So tell me about your 1L grades...Can you explain what happened?" I can say "Whew, it's a long story. So, I wrote a book about it. In fact, I actually brought it with me today. Here's a free copy." Then I would suavely pull out the book from my lap and slide it across the table. He'd read the entire thing aloud, laughing and crying with me as he learned about my story. Then he'd close the book dramatically with tears in his eyes and offer me a job on the spot. But that's not what this book is really about, and that, unfortunately, is not the real reason I wrote it.

I wrote *Underdog* because I wanted to let every law student know that although grades may seem like everything, although it may seem as though your entire future hinges upon your GPA, and although it may be hard to listen to or believe others when they say otherwise, you can have a poor GPA, a failed project, or a gut punch of a setback and still be successful in life. So long as you keep your head up and follow the advice of those who've survived scenarios just as bad as—or perhaps even worse than—yours at the current moment.

This book is about telling that advice and the stories of those I learned from throughout my second year of law school. Through the help of the incredible, self-starting, passionate, and, above all else, persevering individuals I've met throughout writing this book, I was able to discover an area of law that I am deeply passionate about: legal technology.

I learned how to innovate and think creatively to find novel solutions to overcome my obstacles. I learned about appreciating the little things in life and the small wins that help keep the momentum to push forward. And, perhaps most importantly, I learned how to build a network of like-minded individuals who I could trust and lean on in times of need.

For anyone out there who is feeling lost, desperate, or hopeless, I hope this book brings you comfort and faith in yourself because we will push through, we will find a way, and we will succeed. We might be the underdogs, but it's not over until we say it is.

CHAPTER 1

MERRY CHRISTMAS

Embers fell to the ground. A yellow glow slowly enveloped the brown leaves snug within their white paper tubes, before consuming them whole and vanishing into the darkness. It was late December, and I was back at home in the suburbs of Audubon, Pennsylvania. Closing my eyes, I could still feel the knots of stress tight between my shoulder blades straining against the base of my neck. I heaved a thick sigh as grey smoke floated into the distance. I headed back into the basement, sliding the screen door closed and shutting the glass door behind me. My senses were on high alert. Something happened. Shifting my eyes back and forth, I paused to identify the sensation I was feeling. For the past week and a half, the entire law school was keeping a watchful eye on the release of fall semester grades.

Nobody knew exactly when they would be posted since the school didn't send out notifications when the grades portal was updated. So, we simply had to wade our way through the pitch-black abyss of uncertainty. "No...It can't be...," I muttered to myself. I stood completely still at the center of my basement floor listening, feeling for some type of indication from the universe. The next thing I knew I was running and hyperventilating like a madman. I dashed up the stairs, ran down the hall, flung the door of the computer room open, and violently slammed my fingers onto the keyboard to type in my USC username and password. The screen lit up. In tiny black print at the top of the grades portal, a message read: "Grades for your class have been posted. Click here to view." My blood ran cold.

The past four months had been the most excruciating months of my life. I, and every other law student at USC, had locked ourselves in the library. Day in, day out. Studying. Briefing case after case. Re-listening to lectures. Furiously revising outlines. Hoping to get an edge, a point, or anything at all over the rest of the class to push my grade up above the curve as much as possible. I started losing hair from the stress. It wasn't severe—there were no bald spots or signs of a receding hairline. But it was definitely thinning and something I worried about and complained to my mom over the phone constantly. Being someone who's hypercritical of his appearance, hair loss did not sit well with me. At all.

Still, I somehow was able to ignore and logic my way out of it by promising myself that it was temporary and would grow back after the first semester. When I got back home for Christmas break, my mom rushed to hug me at the airport before immediately demanding to see the top of my head. Bowing down so as to allow for a thorough investigation, I could hear my mom mumbling to herself as she combed her fingers across my scalp. "It's okay. Not too bad," she said to me in Mandarin. "It is good for young man to lose hair. Means you are working hard." That was definitely not very accurate medical advice. Still, I prayed that Mom was right—that the stress and pain I endured those four endless months were worth it.

I took a deep breath as though it was the last bid for oxygen I'd have for the rest of my life and clicked the message. The screen flashed and a grid of numbers came up. Grades at USC Gould appeared chronologically from highest to lowest in the class. Each student had a unique exam ID number, so no one knew anyone else's score except for their own, which would appear highlighted on the screen. Looking up and down the screen, there was no yellow highlighted bar in sight. I kept scrolling.

At the top of the page, the highest score for contracts was displayed prominently: 4.4 (A+). "Wow," I exclaimed, "I wonder who got that." I continued to scroll. 3.6 (A-). There were a bunch of those. Maybe nine or ten. Still no highlighted bar. 3.4...3.3. I stopped scrolling. A wave of despair flushed through my veins, extinguishing the effects of the cigarette I finished earlier. The highest grade I could have gotten in contracts at this point was a 3.2 (B) and the lowest a 2.5 (C+). But it didn't matter. To be competitive, according to the career service counselors, I had to at least have a 3.5, if I wanted to do big law—which I did. My other grades were all similarly low, and I was hoping—praying—that maybe I had miraculously done phenomenally in this one class—the class I had studied the most for and felt so confident walking out of. I scrolled one last time. 3.2. I exhaled. After an entire semester of suffering, my highest grade was a B. I wasn't going to do big law. In fact, I'd be lucky if I could get a job at all.

I looked out the window. It had started snowing. You didn't see snow in LA, but it was commonplace in Audubon during the winter. The dark, barren trees in my backyard extended their scraggly tendrils toward the sky in stark contrast to the white, cloudless background. The branches like emaciated fingers begging the heavens for a morsel of sustenance. *"This can't be the end,"* I thought to myself. All that work...for nothing? Was it time for me to pack it up? To move back home with my parents and find a job in Philly? I walked into my bedroom adjacent to the computer room and lay down on my springy mattress, a miserable heap. "I can't keep going on like this," I repeated to myself over and over again as I dozed off.

I woke up in the middle of the night. The air in the house was still, like death, and my family was fast asleep. I got up from the bed slowly, like a corpse rising from its coffin. It was cold. Unsure if I had forgotten to close the basement door, I shivered as I walked downstairs, using my iPhone flashlight to guide me. After seeing the door was locked, I made my way to the kitchen. The refrigerator started humming, startling me for a moment. I entered the living room and walked past the mantel above the fireplace. It was lined with framed graduation pictures from Emory taken about six months ago. I saw my face beaming in the photos, my graduation gown adorned with a golden emblem with a torch and trumpet emblazoned on its face. I received the emblem for successfully completing and defending my honors thesis toward my Chinese major. It was a 116-page essay about a book written by an obscure Jesuit missionary who traveled from Italy to China to convert the Ming Chinese literati. I could do all that...but I couldn't get above a B in law school. I shook my head in disappointment. I knew I had to stop wallowing, but everything seemed so devoid of hope.

My professors might as well have gone ahead and purchased tombstones, one for each of my dreams and aspirations. I trudged up the stairs and down the corridor back to my bedroom, dragging my feet the entire way. I quickly changed into my pajamas and crawled into bed. This was my coffin. I closed my eyes and imagined each of my professors attending my wake. Each of them walked up to my casket to give their condolences. My civil procedure professor's face appeared. She leaned down and whispered softly, "Maybe success in life just wasn't within your jurisdiction." I opened my eyes and scowled back at the empty corner of my bedroom. Pulling the sheets over my head, I shut my eyes as tightly as possible. I knew I was being dramatic. But given the circumstances, maybe it was justified.

The next morning, I woke up to a white glow emanating through my gossamer curtains. I got out of bed to take a look at my front yard and saw the entire lawn had transformed overnight into a white oasis. The pain of seeing my grades last night was still pulsing through me. It was like a mix of anger and exhaustion enveloping me—fire and sludge bogging me down yet keeping me in a hyper-alert state. I felt like I was a race car driver, except instead of speeding forward, I had one foot on the gas pedal and the other on the brakes. I wanted to change and motivate myself to do better, but at the same time, I just felt so crushed and hopeless.

The door creaked open. "Hello? Are you okay?" It was my mom. "Yeah, I'm fine," I responded flatly. My mom had always been there for me. Whether it was getting a B- in Calculus, getting deferred from Washington University in St. Louis my senior year of high school, or getting twenty-one stitches in my jaw from a bicycle accident, my mom always came to me with her full support. The problem was, sometimes, no matter how well-intentioned a person can be, they don't always strike the right chords when trying to comfort others.

"Feeling bad about grade? Don't worry too much! B is good. People say B-students aren't too egotistical—they are humble in the workplace. So maybe people will want to hire you even more," she said with a chuckle.

"Yeah. Maybe." I replied, not really wanting to engage or explain how big law and OCI worked.

"Don't be sad!" she continued, adding, "When Mom sees you sad, Mom gets sad too."

Yup, there it was. The ultimate Asian American immigrant parent trope: guilt. I shouldn't feel sad because by feeling sad for myself, I was making other people around me sad too. So, I had to force myself to be happy. Even when I felt like my life was falling apart.

"I'll try. I just want to be alone right now," I responded flatly.

"Okay. Food is ready downstairs whenever you want to eat breakfast," she said before closing the door and making her way downstairs.

As I listened to the footsteps fade away down the corridor, I plopped myself back onto my bed and screamed into my pillow. I couldn't keep wallowing. I had to figure out a path forward. I picked up my phone and flipped through a list of podcasts. "Something inspirational," I thought to myself, "Something that'll give me some clarity." I came across one that caught my eye: Angela Lee Duckworth's *TED* talk on her book *Grit: The Power of Passion and Perseverance*.[1] Putting on my headphones, I lay down and closed my eyes as Angela began speaking.

She spoke in a soft yet confident tone. Her voice was soothing, but I could tell she was fervent about the topic she was discussing. I looked her up later and found out she was Asian American, which made sense because "Lee"—what I thought was her middle name—was her maiden name. Angela Lee Duckworth was the Christopher H. Browne Distinguished Professor of Psychology at the University of Pennsylvania. She was forty-nine years old, grew up in Cherry Hill, New Jersey, and published her first book, *Grit: The Power of Passion and Perseverance*, back in 2016. In her book, Angela describes grit as passion and perseverance for long-term goals.[2]

During the particular podcast I was listening to, she was actually speaking in front of an audience. She was wearing a black and white floral-print dress with thigh-high leather boots. She spoke eloquently—there was a clear beginning, middle, and end to her message, and she conveyed her points systematically with precision.

"I started studying kids and adults in all kinds of super challenging settings, and [...] one characteristic emerged as a significant predictor of success. And it wasn't social intelligence. It wasn't good looks, physical health, and it wasn't IQ. It was grit."[3]

1   *TED*, "Grit: the power of passion and perseverance," May 9, 2013, video, 6:12.
2   "About Angela," Angela Duckworth, accessed September 3, 2020.
3   Leah Fessler, "'You're No Genius': Her Father's Shutdowns Made Angela Duckworth a World Expert on Grit," *Quartz*, March 26, 2018.

She kept repeating that word throughout her talk—grit. Grit. Grit. "What the hell is grit?" At some point, I dozed off, but that word kept echoing in my head. What was she even talking about?

Somehow, I woke up to the sound of myself repeating "grit" over and over again. I went on her website and found a brief description:

"One way to think about grit is to consider what grit isn't. Grit isn't talent. Grit isn't luck. Grit isn't how intensely, for the moment, you want something. Instead, grit is about having what some researchers call an 'ultimate concern'–a goal you care about so much that it organizes and gives meaning to almost everything you do. And grit is holding steadfast to that goal. Even when you fall down. Even when you screw up. Even when progress toward that goal is halting or slow."[4]

Hm. This was a really profound quandary. What, in my life, was my ultimate concern? What was a goal that I cared about so much that it gave meaning to everything I did and allowed me to get back up every time I failed?

I googled Angela Duckworth again hoping to find what her own ultimate concern was and found the transcript of an interview she had with *Quartz*. After skimming the article, I jotted down three key points I took away from her responses:

First, she explained that people who had a "metacognitive" understanding of themselves were likely to be successful in

---

4   Ibid.

life because they were able to look at themselves and understand what they were doing well and what they were not doing well. Eventually, these were the people who would be able to mediate their weaknesses and raise their strengths. On the other hand, people who lacked self-awareness wouldn't grow. These people might be okay on certain dimensions but would never improve in the long run.[5]

I reflected for a moment on what she said. Growing up, I was made abundantly aware of my shortcomings. I was the kid who could never pay attention in class. I'd get distracted by the most minute disturbances. A fly buzzing above my head. The dripping sounds from a nearby faucet. A classmate breathing through his nostrils when he definitely could've made less noise through his mouth. In the third grade, my teacher, Ms. Yarosh, recommended to my parents that I be assigned a special needs counselor to help me stay on task and complete my work at school.

I distinctly remembered the following week, a lady dressed in a cardigan, needlepoint glasses, and two-inch heels followed me around from classroom to classroom, repeating everything my teachers said in my ear. I could still recall the beginning of my world geography class when Ms. Yarosh told us all to take out our handout from the previous class. My counselor leaned down and whispered, "Do you have it?" to which an angry eight-year-old child with crooked wire frame glasses stared back and replied dramatically: "Yes. Yes, I do have it."

---

5   Ibid.

I was plenty aware of my weaknesses. And while I've definitely improved my ability to focus on and follow through with my daily tasks, I am still a bit scatterbrained. In the context of law school, that was probably one of my biggest drawbacks. When learning the law, the coursework isn't necessarily dense, but it is quite voluminous. And it takes an incredible amount of organization, diligence, and focus to stay on top of everything. That level of discipline was something I definitely needed to continue developing.

The second point Angela made was the importance of small wins. She explained how, while accomplishing seemingly mundane or unpraiseworthy tasks may seem pointless, they actually serve as crucial confidence builders. They are milestones reminding you that you're on the right path. This makes sense because human beings are emotional creatures. We need to be praised, and we don't learn very well when there's no feedback. She provided an example of her work as a manager for a team. After the conclusion of each project, each member would provide the group with two pieces of feedback—one positive and one constructive. She called the positive feedback the "IWEW" or the "It Was Effective When" and the constructive critique an "NTT," which stands for "Next Time Try."[6]

I furrowed my brow. This point really struck at the heart of why I felt so despondent in law school. The thing that made it so different from any of the other academic challenges I'd faced was that there was so little feedback. We read case after case and never knew where we stood among our peers or in

---

6   Ibid.

the eyes of our professors. The only time we were evaluated was on the final exam, which was worth the entirety of our semester GPA. It frustrated me immensely.

The third point was the notion of having an "I'll Show You" mentality. She explained that it's typically a mindset in response to someone telling you that "you cannot." When the coach says you're not on the team or you're not good enough, "I'll show you" essentially says "I'll prove you wrong." She cited Bill McRaven, a retired United States Navy admiral, who explained that he would tell an officer who he really believed in, during weed-out challenges, "prove me wrong," which was in the same vein as "I'll show you."[7] In short, those who were gritty possessed a type of "Underdog Mentality" that motivated them to keep going.

That third point resonated most with me because I've always had this innate desire to prove myself ever since I was a toddler. My mom would tell me stories about how when I was born, not only was I the fattest and loudest baby in the nursery, I also had a habit of fighting with the nurses, slapping away their hands and wriggling my fat fists at them whenever it was time for them to change my diaper. Throughout my childhood, whether it was passive aggressively replying to my guidance counselor in elementary school to prove that I didn't need her assistance or continually taking (and failing) the exam to get into the gifted section in middle school to prove that I was smart enough, I had always fought to assert myself and to make sure people knew my worth.

---

7   Ibid.

Based on the sum of all my experiences that led me to law school, there was no doubt in my mind that I had an Underdog Mentality. Though it waxed and waned, I knew the moment my third-grade special needs counselor whispered in my ear, asking whether I had my geography handout, that I had something to prove.

I closed the tab of Angela's article and rolled over in my bed. I didn't know what my ultimate concern was, but it was comforting to know that I was on the right track based on the fact that I had spent a significant amount of time already reasoning through the points Angela made. I knew I could use her insight as a guide to help figure out what my top-level goal was. What was I all about? What endgame did I want so badly that I'd be willing to go all in to accomplish it?

My mom's voice surged and vibrated up the staircase into my room: "Get up! Breakfast is ready. Come to eat!"

I rushed downstairs. I knew in the back of my mind that Angela's words would follow me throughout the rest of my time in law school. This was only the beginning of my journey, and, whether I was ready for it or not, I had to put my best foot forward and give it my all.

CHAPTER 2

BONAFIDE CHICKEN DINNER

"Well, I have to say, this was a phenomenal presentation. I mean, Cajun Classics—you guys clearly did your research. Loved your big idea. I mean, really great job," the CEO's voice echoed throughout the room. The audience erupted with applause. He continued: "Okay, give us some time to deliberate, and we'll ask all the teams to come back in once we've decided on the winner." The five of us walked out of the room, heads and spirits high. As I entered the lobby, the sound of water splashing from the fountain outside the presentation room reverberated throughout the surrounding glass walls. Every few seconds, the cascading waters spelled out the words "Coca-Cola" in the logo's iconic font before disappearing into the tiled basin below. Adjacent to the fountain was a large mural made of aluminum bottle caps taken from the tops of glass soda bottles, carefully pieced together to form a gigantic picture of a tin coke can.[8]

---

8   "BBA marketing class gives unique real-world experience to students," *Emory Business*, accessed on August 31, 2020.

I gazed outside the large glass windows across the courtyard. Just by the doorway to the building was a monitor presenting a slideshow of messages. The screen flashed in bold letters "Welcome Goizueta Business School Students" before transitioning to another slide showing another message, "Welcome Restaurant Brands International & Popeyes Louisiana Kitchen." I couldn't stop beaming. It was 2018, and I was wrapping up my senior year at Emory. How often did an undergraduate business school student get to work on a marketing proposal for executives of Popeyes Louisiana Kitchen at the Coke Headquarters in Atlanta? My teammates and I had just spent the spring semester pouring ourselves, heart and soul, into the presentation we just gave, and we completely knocked it out of the park. We were eager to know our results. Suddenly my phone rang. The area code read "213." It had to be USC. I quickly picked up and moved to a secluded area down the hall.

"Hello?" I said timidly.

A bright voice shot back through the line: "Hey, Jesse! This is Jessica calling from USC. I have some news for you, are you ready?"

"Yes, of course!" I shouted reflexively, trying to match the voice's energy.

"We'd like to offer you a spot in USC Gould School of Law's JD Class of 2021. Are you interested?" she responded cheerily.

"A-Absolutely!" I shouted back.

Before I even finished, the voice shot back once more: "Fantastic! I'll send over your offer letter in the next hour or so. Welcome to the Trojan family, Jesse! Cheers!"

The dial tone rang. I stared at the ground for a few seconds, my mouth agape, trying to comprehend what had just happened. I made my way down the hall, back to the lobby. As I entered, I saw the judges were standing in front of the class. Suddenly, my teammates all started screaming and jumping up and down.

"We won! I can't believe it, we won!" they yelled.

I quickly ran to join our victory screech. We embraced each other for a group hug.

"I can't believe it...I—this is amazing," my teammate Crystal said, as her eyes started welling up with tears of joy.

"You guys ready to turn up?" Sanjay yelled, unable to contain his enthusiasm.

"Hell yes!" we replied as a chorus.

We quickly piled into Sanjay's car and were on our way back to campus, where our entire marketing class was having an end-of-the-semester party to celebrate presenting our proposals. "Sanjay, turn it up!" I yelled from the back. The iconic guitar riff of "Don't Fear the Reaper" by Blue Öyster Cult began reverberating throughout the car. The hot Atlanta sun beat down on the car's red tinted exterior. We opened the moon roof, letting the rays flood over us. Another team's car pulled up beside us at the traffic light, and we exchanged lighthearted jeers. As we drove down the highway, the Atlanta skyline shrank into the distance until it became a miniature LEGO set. Buck Dharma went into the outro, as Sanjay turned the volume even higher. I couldn't stop smiling. Everything that I had dreamt of was coming true. It was perfect. Absolutely perfect.

"I need to pinch myself," I said to Crystal. "This *has* to be a dream," I added heartily.

She stared back blankly for a few seconds before smiling and responding cheerily: "Ha-ha, don't pinch yourself. You'll ruin it."

Her words caused a chill to sweep through my entire body. It felt like a gust of snowflakes had permeated my skin, blustering from my scalp all the way down to the base of my spine. My senses immediately shot back into high alert. I realized in that moment what was happening. This all felt too good to be true...because it was.

Blue Öyster's guitar riff suddenly sank into a lower octave. The lead singer's voice began to warp like it was playing from a record player doused in molasses and battery acid. I noticed the car seat was beginning to stick to my suit. My hand sank into the polyester arm rest beside me. I tried yanking it out, but the more I squirmed, the further down it sank.

I yelled over the music, "Hey, Sanjay, what's going on with your car."

No response.

I paused before yelling again: "…Sanjay?"

I looked up to see if he was listening to me and immediately flinched. Sanjay had been replaced by a hooded figure.

"Wait…W-who are you?…Where are you taking us?" I asked, my voice trembling in fear.

"Us?" he replied inquisitively. His voice sounded distorted, almost demonic.

"Yeah, us…," I responded, as I slowly turned my head to the left.

I froze. The color in my face receded. Icicles shot through my veins, as my body temperature dropped. Crystal was nowhere to be found. The backseat was empty. I was alone.

"Your friends all got jobs, Jesse. Crystal's working at Saatchi & Saatchi, Isaac's at Booz Allen, Sanjay's at Simon-Kucher, and Julia's at Edelman. You're all alone now," he sneered. Then he cackled. But not like a fake Disney villain's cackle. No—a deep, guttural cackle. A cackle that could cause an entire crowd's hair to stand on end. I shivered in fear and disgust.

"Oh, there's one now. Why don't you say hi?" he said coyly.

I looked out the window. It was Crystal, speeding down the highway in the lane beside us in a pink Corvette. A yellow glow emanated from the passenger seat. I squinted my eyes to get a better look. It was gold. Bars of gold stacked from the base of her seat to the height of the car.

I pounded at the window. "Crystal! Crystal! Help me! Please!"

She sped ahead into the distance until she was just a dot on the horizon.

"Don't worry. She wasn't ignoring you. She was just focusing on moving ahead in life. You know she has a five-year plan to get married, have kids, and move to the suburbs, right?" he said menacingly.

"No, I—this is false imprisonment, a violation of Georgia's penal code," I stuttered.

He cackled his blood-curdling cackle again and sneered, "Well, you can't sue me. Your GPA isn't high enough to be taken seriously!"

Suddenly, gold bars started growing out of the car door adjacent to me. They fell into my lap. As more and more appeared, they started getting hotter in temperature, until they began burning into my flesh.

"Holy shit!" I shouted, wincing in pain.

The bars suddenly turned black and red numbers appeared on each of them. There were six bars, each of them with glowing red numbers rapidly changing and flashing before my eyes. Finally, the numbers stopped.

Engraved in blood red text, the black bars read: "$10,000."

"Negative $10,000 each," the hooded figure said ominously.

"That's how much you're gonna owe each year from the choice you made, Jesse."

I shrieked back at him: "How long is that going to take to pay off?"

He shook his head, heaved an exasperated sigh, and replied, "Maybe you should take a corporate finance class."

I shrieked even louder. Tears cascaded down my cheeks, and I began to hyperventilate.

I continued to shriek at the top of my lungs, as the car started melting from under me. Through the large holes of the car's melted polyester and aluminum, I could see the yellow lines of the road flashing rapidly beneath me. I began to wail. The Atlanta skyscrapers looming outside the car windows began morphing into grotesque pillars of black sludge. As they dissolved, I could hear fire alarms ringing from all of them at once.

"This isn't real. This isn't real," I sobbed loudly, as I stuck my pointer finger from my free hand into my ear and shut my eyes.

"Turn it off!" the hooded figure's demonic voice boomed.

"Don't yell at me, I'm trying to wake myself up," I wailed back between hiccups and sobs. He shook his head out of frustration.

"Stop crying and turn it off!" he boomed back again.

I inhaled dramatically and screamed at the top of my lungs, "You're sitting closer to the radio, why don't you turn it off!"

Removing my hand from my ear, I pinched a piece of skin on my thigh between my index finger and thumb, applying as much pressure against my flesh as I could muster. A red-hot stab of pain tore away the fabric of the hellish dreamscape. I winced. The chaotic imagery before me instantly evaporated into a white emptiness. Ripping apart the crusty rheum that had sealed my eyelids shut overnight, I opened my eyes and shot straight up in my bed at a ninety-degree angle, like a malfunctioning folding chair.

My phone was vibrating on my nightstand, flailing in desperation like a fish out of water. I looked down and saw my shirt and pants were completely drenched in a cold sweat. I looked around the room and spotted a disgruntled face glaring at me.

"Dude, you were crying all night. Again. Could you at least remember to turn your alarm off?" my roommate moaned at me with his eyes half-open.

Grabbing the phone off the nightstand, I quickly put the device on silent before apologizing and making a beeline to the bathroom to splash my face with some cold water. Of course, it was a dream. My team didn't win the case competition for Popeyes in 2018, USC never called me when I was admitted to law school, and "Don't Fear the Reaper" was certainly not celebratory music. I looked up at my reflection in the mirror. A ghastly face with craters beneath its eyes stared grimly back at me. What a bleak way to start the day.

A week earlier, I had gotten my 1L spring semester grades back. That morning, I opened my laptop and heard a thousand screams from my Chinese ancestors yelling at me in Mandarin, "You let us down! You lazy shit, how could you!" They were lower than they had been the previous semester. My cumulative GPA was a 3.06, and, a couple days later, I got an email saying that I had to be placed in the Additional Graduation Requirement (AGR) program, along with all students who had a GPA of 3.1 or below at the conclusion of their first year. As part of the program, I had to meet with an academic advisor twice a semester during my 2L and 3L years, as well as take all bar courses for a letter grade. Meaning, I wouldn't be allowed to opt for credit/no credit grading for any of the tougher classes in case I wanted to slack off. I didn't mind the additional help. But the blow to my ego and self-esteem left me in tatters. Luckily, I secured a summer clerkship at the Los Angeles Center for Law and Justice (LACLJ) located in East Los Angeles prior to my grades coming out.

After brushing my teeth and getting dressed, I made my way to the Metro station behind my apartment complex. As I ran down the stairs and out the back entrance, a wave of hot June air walloped me in the face. Immediately, I started sweating, moisture collecting in the space between my back and book bag. There was no time to complain. I kept up my pace.

The Blue Line pulled up to the tracks adjacent to me, and I made a dash to cross the intersection to meet it before the timer went out. I quickly tapped my MetroLink at the steel kiosk and bolted to an open seat inside the air-conditioned train, breathing a sigh of relief as I sat down. Made it. It was a ninety-minute commute from my apartment near USC's campus near downtown LA to LACLJ's office on Whittier in the valley. But for now, I could relax. At least for the next thirty minutes until I had to switch to the Silver Line. I put on my headphones and switched on an episode of "Work Life" by Adam Grant. The Metro sped down the tracks as Adam began his lecture.

Working at a nonprofit law firm over the summer was a much -needed respite from the onslaught of work of the 1L year. It was also a reality check. I was working with clients who had fallen through the cracks into America's dark underbelly. These were people who had been trafficked in the United States and forced to do manual labor without pay. Some were victims of domestic violence, desperately seeking an escape from abusive partners for themselves and for their children. Many had nowhere else to turn; with no money or family in the US, LACLJ was the last place they could turn to for help.

I distinctly recall one instance a client came in with her son. They were Chinese and couldn't speak English very well. They reminded me of my mom and me. When they walked in, it looked as though they hadn't changed their clothes in weeks. She wore a sweater with holes in it despite the hot Los Angeles weather, and he wore an oversized T-shirt and jeans with stains on them. The mother took out several pieces of crumpled paper from her purse, asking us to help her apply for a T-Visa. I was the only Mandarin-speaking law clerk at the time, and I spent the afternoon collecting information from them and helping them fill out the forms. They told me they had been staying at a local homeless shelter. Her son was studying for the SATs and planning to apply for schools within the University of California system.

When I asked him to sign his name on one of the forms, I noticed his nails were untrimmed and his hair was greasy and speckled with dandruff. He had bored a hole through his sneakers, and the fabric of his sock protruded from the heel. When we finished filling out the application, the mother thanked me profusely. She was ecstatic that she finally found someone who could speak Mandarin, and they both left beaming. As soon as they left, I walked to the bathroom to wipe away a few tears before making my way back to my desk.

A few minutes later, another law clerk, Erica, walked by cheerily and asked if I wanted to get some food. I immediately agreed and logged out of my desktop. I was starving. We made our way down the street to a row of restaurants. It was a mix of local mom-and-pops and franchises, ranging from Tacos Baja to Starbucks and KFC.

As we walked down the row to view our options for sustenance, we spotted a bright red and orange building, vaguely reminiscent of the New Orleans French Quarter architecture style, sitting in the distance. The exterior was complete with a green antique wooden balcony and red-shingled eaves, starkly contrasting the smooth yellow facade. Painted *trompe l'oeil* adorned the walls, giving the illusion of green vases sitting at the foot of each of the building's four corners. The restaurant completely stood out among its competitors in the vicinity, as if imported directly from Louisiana, not knowing it was in the wrong neighborhood, the wrong city, and the wrong state.

The front of the building had a sign spelling out, in a bold, uneven font, "Popeyes Louisiana Kitchen." We walked in, and I immediately heard the familiar voice of my client.

"We please get bone-fed chicken dinner?" she asked in broken English.

"A what, ma'am?" the cashier responded in an irritated tone.

"BONE-FED CHICKEN, PLEASE," her son echoed loudly.

"Bonafide chicken, you mean?" she replied, with increased irritation.

"Yes, thank you, please," he responded quickly, eager to end the conversation.

Erica and I took our meals to go. As we exited the restaurant, I looked back to see the mother smiling as she watched her son take the first bite out of a drumstick. They were celebrating. They didn't have enough money for a proper pair of shoes or a bed to sleep in. But they were happy with what they had, and they were paving the way for a new life.

I smiled to myself as we walked back to the office. Even though my work at LACLJ didn't feel groundbreaking or as intense as what I expected legal work would be like, and even though it wasn't as sexy or glamorous as presenting to Popeyes and Coca-Cola executives, the work was still significant. I made a difference in others' lives, and that made me feel good about myself. I opened my paper box of fried chicken at my desk and stared at the flaky golden-brown crust. All those months I poured into marketing this fried chicken…and I never saw someone as happy as that mom and son sharing their Bonafide Chicken Dinner to celebrate applying for a visa. I took a bite. It was good, as expected. But maybe, just maybe, the hooded kidnapper from my dream was wrong. Maybe I hadn't made the wrong choice.

CHAPTER 3

LIKE WATER

———

I took a deep breath and walked through the sliding glass doors of the USC Hotel. The lobby was cramped with familiar faces, all of them rising 2Ls and 3Ls. I walked up to the second floor and peered down the corridor. The hallway was filled to the brim with students sitting in chairs lining the walls. Every so often, the door to one of the hotel rooms would open, a student would walk out, shut the door behind him, and let the person seated just outside the door know that the interviewer would call them in after a few minutes.

I held on tightly to my binders as I sat down next to a classmate. I had custom-made a binder of materials for each of the firms I was interviewing with, including my résumé, cover letter, and transcripts, complete with a cover with the law firm's logo emblazoned at the top. My thought process was, if I was going down at OCI, I was going down fighting.

OCI, or "on-campus interviewing," is a part of the law firm recruitment process when partners and associates from law firms visited certain law schools across the nation to interview students for summer associate or full-time positions.[9] It's a highly routinized, almost ritualistic, tradition that took place each year. Like an annual square dance. Except, there's no music...or laughter...or joy. And instead of a partner who dances with you, you got one who grills you with questions. And instead of receiving a standing ovation, you receive permanent emotional scarring. But if you were lucky, you might get a callback for a second-round interview, which would make the entire hellish experience somehow worth it.

At USC, recruiters and partners from competitive, large law firms with 500 or more attorneys, including Sidley Austin LLP, Jones Day, and Kirkland & Ellis LLP, fly in from all across the country to set up shop at the USC Hotel located right across the street from the law school for a week toward the end of the summer.[10] Students enter their names into a quasi-lottery system online. Everyone gets a certain number of bid points, which they allocate among the firms they'd like to interview with; the more points allocated to a firm, the more likely the student would land an interview slot with them. If you were one of the more aggressive participants of OCI, you probably started networking far in advance and likely got an early screener interview or had your name pre-selected by a recruiter.[11] None of this really mattered to me, though, because of the soul-crushing feedback I kept receiving from career counselors that my grades were too

9   "Everything you need to know about OCI: on-campus interviewing," *ABA for Law Students: Before the Bar (BB)*, accessed August 31, 2020.

10   "ABA Employment Summary," USC Gould School of Law, accessed August 31, 2020.

11   "The Phases of OCI: Phase 2 – Preselection & On-Campus Interviews," University of Denver: Sturm College of Law - Career Connection, accessed September 1, 2020.

low and that I was unlikely to get any callbacks. Still, I was determined to just give it a shot.

I sat down on one of the chairs outside of the room I was assigned for my interview. Turning to my side to make small talk with whomever was sitting beside me, I saw a familiar face. "Hey James, what's up!" I said lightheartedly. He smiled back. James was in my Super Section all throughout 1L year. Basically, during the first year of law school at USC, the incoming class was broken down into three Super Sections: A-E, F-J, and K-O. Students within the same Super Section took all the core 1L courses together. Then, each of those Supers were further broken down into small sections, with around twelve or thirteen students each. Students in each small section took Legal Writing & Research together, in addition to the other core classes with the rest of the Super Section.

James was a few years older than I was and had worked in Silicon Valley as a legal specialist at Google after graduating from Loyola Marymount University with a Bachelor of Arts in political science. He looked incredibly put together in his navy suit and freshly trimmed beard. His light brown hair was styled in such a way that it was perfectly coiffed yet still appeared as though it had naturally fallen into place, as if to demonstrate to the law firms that his precision and dedication extended to his appearance as well as his work. James had a bit of time before his next interview, so we ended up chatting about life. It was his twelfth interview of the day and, though he admitted he was tired, he hardly looked it. After all, he was no stranger to dealing with an unfriendly schedule.

"I've been here for maybe six or six-and-a-half hours now, but at least I don't have to spend four of those hours commuting," he said with a laugh. He explained that while working at Google, he commuted a little over two hours each way from his home in Marin county to his office in Mountain View. Every morning, he would get up at 5:45, get on a bus at around 6:20, and then arrive to work at around 8:30. In spite of all the perks of working at a company at Google, the long treks each day were frustrating and wore him out. I could understand James's pain to an extent.

My ninety-minute commute to LACLJ definitely took a toll on my mental health. I recalled glancing at a study published in the *Journal of Transport & Health* by a researcher named Xize Wang that concluded that longer commuting time was associated with higher rates of depression.[12] Traffic delays and poor access to transit were the primary triggering factors.[13] Luckily for me, my commute was only for a summer. In stark contrast, James had commuted more than four hours per day for a whopping three years. And he was traveling to and from one of the most congested places in California.

Astonished at the thought of spending almost a quarter of my waking hours on a bus for five days a week, I asked, "Did you ever consider moving closer to work? I mean, what made you stick with that kind of schedule?" "I saw it as an investment," he replied. The entire time James was at Google and even

---

12   Xize Wang, "Commute patterns and depression: Evidence from eleven Latin American cities," *Journal of Transport & Health* Volume 14 (September 2019): 2-13.

13   Ibid.

throughout his time as an undergraduate, James had been thinking about law school.

He was investing in his future and wanted to set himself up as well as he could financially. So, he saw the perks of living at home and not having to pay for rent or food as worth putting up with the ungodly amount of traveling his job required. Still it was tough on James, physically and mentally. "I didn't have much of a social life. And I definitely developed some back issues from having to sit upright for so long and for so many days in a row," he admitted. He mostly spent the weekends vegging out and resting in preparation for the upcoming week. And when he began studying for the LSAT (Law School Admission Test), his downtime became even more scarce.

One positive outcome that came from James's experience was that it taught him how to let go of things that were out of his control. He explained how at some point he had to come to terms with the fact that the commute was going to suck no matter what and that complaining wasn't going to change anything. "Whether there would be more or less traffic—it didn't really make a difference. I was going to be on that bus for four or more hours, so I just made peace with it and tried to conserve as much energy as I could. And that meant not spending time being mad about the inevitable," he said with a shrug.

So, James turned his commutes into what he called "prep time." On the ride to Mountain View, he would listen to podcasts about setting healthy work-life boundaries, boot up his computer, and try his best to mentally prepare himself for the day. On the journeys back home, he would typically unwind by listening to his favorite music or calling up a family member to catch up.

James's approach reminded me of a philosophy I had studied back at Emory. During my senior year of college, I wrote a thesis on the Confucian Classics and the concept of wú wéi (无为) within Daoism (道教).[14] The premise of wú wéi was essentially that one's actions should be effortless or free-flowing.[15] Bruce Lee famously explained it as "being like water." While water was typically regarded as a submissive or weak element, its power lay in its fluidity, allowing it to erode even the toughest and most rigid stones. In other words, being adaptable and malleable to changing circumstances could often times be the most effective way to overcome difficult obstacles.[16] This was precisely what James did during those lengthy commutes. With a gentle persistence and compliance, he worked around the obstacle in front of him and filled his time on the bus with things he enjoyed.

But letting go didn't come naturally for James, and it was something he was still getting the hang of even throughout OCI. "I think I'm really prone to hyper-analysis, and certain situations can easily trigger that," he said. He explained how he was feeling quite a bit of pressure at OCI, largely due to the uncertainty of the entire process. While his life at Google

14 Wang, Jesse, "The Confucian Christian: A Study on the Rhetorical and Ideological Accommodation of Alfonso Vagnone's Illustrations of the Grand Dao (達道紀言), Emory Theses and Dissertations (ETD) Repository: 36-37.

15 Ibid.

16 "The Best is Like Water," China Heritage: The Wairarapa Academy for New Sinology, accessed September 3, 2020.

wasn't perfect, he still enjoyed working there and, by leaving to attend law school, he sacrificed a steady income and stability. In his mind, if he didn't get an offer for a position in big law, then maybe coming to USC wasn't as good an investment as he originally thought it would be. As a result, the pressure was triggering his hyper-analytical instincts, and they had reached a fever pitch when he received an email earlier: "Before you got here, I was literally obsessing over a smiley face I got in an email from an attorney I spoke to a couple weeks ago. A smiley face!" He shook his head incredulously.

I could tell he knew obsessing over something so minute was silly, but that didn't make it any less difficult for him to fight his inclination for over-analysis. He even made a bulleted list of the possible messages that a smiley face could have signaled. Did it mean the law firm liked him? Were they just being nice? Was it an accident? The stark reality was, however, that James could never know for certain what the attorneys were thinking and whether he would receive an offer from them or not. And that lack of control, combined with the weight of everything he had sacrificed to come to Los Angeles for law school, thrust James down a dark rabbit hole of anxiety and fear.

I patted him on the shoulder sympathetically. I knew I personally didn't have a shot because of my grades. But here was someone who had worked tirelessly for three years at Google, sacrificed a well-paying and enjoyable job to come to law school, had solid grades, and had a significant shot at getting an offer from at least one of the firms interviewing at the hotel. It took me by surprise to see someone like James experiencing similar, if not more intense, feelings of apprehension as I was.

Grasping for the silver lining, I asked, "Have you done anything recently that's helped you cope with the anxiety? I mean, are there any similar coping mechanisms you've been using, like when you were dealing with the long commutes back then?" He looked up and replied brightly, "Yeah, I've been texting friends and family throughout the day to vent. I think that's helped. But I also have been trying this new thing called setting 'worry times.' I heard about it in a podcast once. I think it's been somewhat useful."

Worry time, as James described, was basically time purposefully set aside during the day that is specifically devoted to obsessing or worrying. It's a technique psychologists have taught to patients undergoing cognitive-behavioral therapy and has been proven to reduce the occurrence of negative intrusive thoughts.[17] The concept was simple: Twice a day, James would set aside two blocks of time, fifteen to twenty minutes each, to worry about a particular problem. He'd sit down in an area where they weren't too many people, adjust his mental magnifying glass, and home in, full steam ahead, on all of the potential disastrous outcomes that he could foresee. The more negative thoughts, the better! The goal was to be as uncomfortable as possible and to review the deepest and darkest thoughts conceivable. However, once that daily "worry time" ran out, James would take a few calming breaths, shake out any lingering tension, and go on about his day. "It takes a lot of practice, but I think it works," he said.

---

17   "Worry," Association for Behavioral and Cognitive Therapies (ABCT), accessed August 31, 2020.

"But how can focusing so intensely on the negatives mitigate your anxiety?" I asked inquisitively. James explained that getting those negative thoughts out in the open was akin to stripping them of their power to surprise and frighten. Once the worst-case scenario lost its novelty, the anxiety associated with it stopped accumulating and eventually waned. "It gets boring after a while," he replied. "I mean, usually the way intrusive thoughts work is they come and go throughout the day. You fight to break free from them, but new make-believe scenarios seem to pop up because our minds are that good at stressing us out. But when we dedicate time to brainstorming horrible potential situations, we become used to it. And so, when they pop up later on in the day, they're not as frightening because it's like, 'Oh, I've already imagined that and made peace with it.'"

Another way to look at James's use of "worry time" could be as an exercise of wú wéi. Instead of fighting his mind's urge to meander or attempting to suppress negative thoughts, he purposefully allowed them to run freely. Like water. Dark thoughts would flood and rinse through the crevices of his mind, washing through every potential diegesis, every possible Freudian slip, and every imagined faux pas. And, once those thoughts cleansed every iota of his dark imagination, James was free. He sank the enemy's most powerful battleship—the element of surprise. Little did the Daoists know that their philosophies would make their way to Western society and be used by law students during OCI. James was doing exactly what Confucius taught his disciples. Paradoxically, by releasing his need for control, James was able to regain it. And, though the technique wasn't perfect, it made his life a bit easier, and that's what mattered.

The door to the room adjacent to us swung open and a student walked out. "They said you can head in," he said in a baritone voice before walking off. I wished James good luck as he disappeared into the room. I still had some time before my first interview, but after chatting with James, I felt much more at peace.

At this juncture, I couldn't change my grades, add any other work experiences to my résumé, or do any more interview preparation. All I could do was go into the room, present myself as best as I could, and be done with it. The door to the other side of me opened. A man in his mid-thirties stepped halfway into the hall and greeted me with a smile, "You must be Jesse. Come on in." I smiled back, grabbed my binders, and walked inside. *"Like water...,"* I thought to myself, *"like water."*

CHAPTER 4

BEST FOOT FORWARD

"Yeah, did you hear? He got like twelve callbacks and flew out to San Francisco for his second round."

"No way. That's amazing. I only got five, but I have my eye on two in particular."

My classmates chattered excitedly as I walked past them and toward the law library. I was happy for them. They all worked really hard and were extremely smart; they deserved it. But deep down, it was hard to escape the smothering sensation of profound inadequacy. Like a demon suffocating me—its tendrils lugging me into the abyss.

The feeling weighed on me throughout the entire fall semester of my second year. I felt like a defective product. Here I was at one of the best law schools in the country, the University of Southern California, and none of the firms I interviewed with—even the smaller ones—wanted to speak with me again. I also felt an overwhelming sense of loneliness, like I was the only one who came away empty-handed. I mean, I suppose people didn't really talk about their failures, so

I wouldn't know whether or not others also didn't get any callbacks, but even knowing that wasn't enough to shake the feeling of ineptitude in the pit of my stomach.

I sat down at an empty study desk. It was the first week of the fall semester, and I had to come up with a game plan for how I was going to keep up the morale and land an interview, let alone a job offer. Reflecting on what Angela had said in her interview about gritty people knowing their strengths and leveraging them to their advantage, I took a moment to catalogue my strengths and jotted down three of what I thought were my greatest ones on a piece of notebook paper:

1. I'm creative
2. I'm extroverted and collaborative
3. I'm highly resourceful[18]

These traits served me well during my time as an undergraduate at Emory University. I was a business and Chinese studies double major and had a ton of group projects and assignments. But law school was a completely different animal. Being extroverted or collaborative hadn't exactly scored me any brownie points.

I remembered during my 1L year I tried desperately to form groups with classmates to outline and review course concepts. Though it worked a few times, it just wasn't sustainable. Almost everything in the 1L curriculum was individual work, and everyone outlined and studied at a different pace.

---

18   Leah Fessler, "'You're No Genius': Her Father's Shutdowns Made Angela Duckworth a World Expert on Grit," *Quartz*, March 26, 2018.

I was always ahead on the material, doing case briefs for every reading a week in advance. Some of my classmates found that intimidating or anxiety provoking because it made them think they were behind. Little did they know, the one who seemed most prepared would perform below average across the board.

I had to think outside the box. There had to be something—a class or an organization—I could join that would allow me to thrive as a creative extrovert in law school. I spent the next two hours in the library, scrolling through Gould's course catalog online and reading description after description. First Amendment…Criminal Procedure…Legal Innovations Lab. My eyes zeroed in on the last one. I immediately clicked the name of the professor who taught the course and, after a quick Google search, found an article describing her work as an associate at Sidley Austin LLP, a large multinational law firm, and her work as the founder of a document automation platform for lawyers, creatively titled "Documate."[19]

Scrolling back to finish reading the course description, I felt butterflies in my stomach. I didn't even fully know exactly what the course was about yet, but somehow, I was certain I was onto something big. According to the course catalog, Legal Innovations Lab was a course in which students formed into groups and developed their own technology-based solution to a legal issue. So, it was sort of like a shark tank for lawyers. At the end of the semester, students presented their projects at the Los Angeles Global Legal Hackathon in front

19   Laurie Rowen, "Meet Dorna Moini: Founder of LegalTech Company Documate," Montage Legal Group, April 29, 2019.

of a panel of start-up founders, attorneys, and others within the Los Angeles legal community.[20]

Finally. Finally, this was my chance. Maybe the possibility of working at a large law firm right out of law school had evaporated, but legal technology was an entirely different field. My mind started swirling with idealized scenarios. I imagined my name and headshot featured on *TIME* magazine's cover—"Jesse Wang: Legal Innovator and Start-up Founder Who Did Below Average in Law School Yet Succeeded Nonetheless." Not the catchiest title, but I had time to work on it. I selected "register" on the screen and attended class the next day. And, within the first week, I was absolutely hooked.

Our class was small, with only nine students, but that just gave us a greater opportunity to get to know each other better and to collaborate. Walking into the tiny room in the library for class every Wednesday evening felt like being in some kind of secret organization. I was a member of the core pro-legal technology lobbying squad, like the team from Miss Sloane, and Professor Moini was Jessica Chastain's character—Elizabeth Sloane. Our mission was to use technology to expand access to justice, by creating more affordable and accessible pathways for vulnerable communities to obtain legal services.

Access to Justice, or A2J for short, wasn't just a clever moniker. It was a mission—a cause in which Professor Moini and the

---

20 "Global Legal Hackathon: World's Largest Legal Hackathon," Global Legal Hackathon, accessed September 3, 2020.

people in our class staunchly believed.[21] On the first day of class, Professor Moini gave a short presentation on the services that her start-up, Documate, provides to clients. She explained that Documate was an online document automation platform that allowed users to create template documents for legal aid organizations, nonprofits, and small businesses that otherwise would not be able to afford attorneys.

Originally, the idea was to create a platform specifically geared toward DV work. Seeing how taxing it was to navigate all of the formalities and routinized workflows DV clients and pro bono attorneys had to put up with, Professor Moini saw that inventing a software that streamlined the process was an innovative solution that would solve an unaddressed legal need. Moreover, from an economic and affordability perspective, the need to create such a platform was intensified by the fact that pro bono legal aid organizations were.

Considering how little legal aid organizations could spend, compared to the vast client demand, implementing such a platform would help reduce costs and make the work much more efficient.

However, the idea didn't really take off initially. One particular issue was the original business model's scalability—the company's ability to expand in size and increase sales. A low-cost, jurisdiction-specific platform just wasn't able to reach the profitability needed to be sustainable. She explained, "We had several legal aid organizations and domestic violence

21 Zorik Pesochinsky, "Leveraging Legal Technology to Improve Access to Justice," *Thomas Reuters Legal Executive Institute*, accessed September 10, 2020.

shelters using our platform, but we were providing our software to them for free to support their work. We also sold the service to consumers at fifteen dollars total, which meant that we were spending much more money acquiring those customers than the sale was covering."

Professor Moini resolved to broaden Documate's reach by making the software more applicable to legal work generally. Elaborating on her revelation that motivated her to make the change, she said, "The 'A-ha' moment, I think, came when we thought of building a platform that users could build on top of. So, instead of just having built-in DV questions, the users could change and alter the text to fit their individual scenarios and connect them to their own custom documents and templates, in any jurisdiction." Expanding Documate's functions across multiple areas of law was a step in the right direction.

The adjustment immediately caught on, as all of the previous legal aid organizations who had reached out before were now interested in the services that could be applied to their areas of legal work. She told our class, "We realized that there was a really big need for technology like the DV automation because so many legal aid organizations and law firms were interested in the concept of the technology itself, rather than our initial, narrow product. So, once we made the platform, it was a much better business model, and we immediately got those initial legal aid orgs and firms onboard as customers. Marketing and strategy are important to build the business, but after we quickly found the product-market fit, Documate has just been growing and adding new features to make the platform into a more robust expert system builder ever since."

Professor Moini ended her presentation by leaving the class with one crucial lesson she learned from her experience founding Documate: "In whatever career you decide to pursue, be sure to get out there and suss out a need—a gap in whatever field or industry you're in that needs filling. Because at the end of the day, success is defined by how much you are able to help those around you. How can you make other people's lives easier? How can you make life more bearable? It's a dual motive, because by providing value to others and to the community at large, you are also helping yourself and building a stronger consumer base. And the key to being able to discover and identify a problem and a solution to it? Networking. I would say the most important thing, for law students at least, is to get out there. Go to events. Meet like-minded individuals. Talk to people who might do similar things as you or who might be good at connecting you with others. When I was in school, I did two hackathons in San Francisco and went to every networking event I could. Also, I didn't have any technical skills, so it was really good for me to connect with engineers at those events. It was by talking to all of these people from diverse backgrounds—attorneys, engineers, clients, legal aid organizations—that I was able to figure out, first, what problem needed to be solved and, second, how I could assemble an all-star team to help me build a solution."

I left class that day filled with verve and determination. Finally, a law professor who understood the importance of social skills—someone who didn't continuously harp on the frustrating sound bite that GPA determines everything in life. It was time for me to leverage my strengths. It was time for me to use my extroversion to my full advantage. It was time to put my best foot forward and fight like my life depended on it.

CHAPTER 5

A BUILDER'S MINDSET

———

I knew Professor Moini's advice was good because it wasn't the first time I had heard that sound bite. The first time was when I was in elementary school. My mom used to constantly remind me to "hang out with the smart kids" because they would motivate me to work harder and improve. She also said that if I spent too much time with losers, they would encourage me to slack off, and I would end up working at McDonalds, to which I'd reply, "At least I'd get free McNuggets!" Notwithstanding her condescension toward fast food workers, she had a point. If I wanted to be successful, the best way to increase my odds was to find people who had similar plans and work with them.

Now, it was time for me to turn that advice into action. A month into the spring semester, I quickly rallied up a few classmates who were, at least vaguely, interested in legal technology and start-ups and founded a new student organization at Gould—the Legal Technology Association (LTA). My thought process was that by bringing in attorneys, start-up counsels, and CEOs of small businesses across the country to speak with students at Gould, I could:

1. Utilize my extroversion to make connections with people who might have valuable advice,
2. Expose students at Gould, myself included, to alternative career paths that lawyers have taken in the legal technology and innovation space, and
3. Demonstrate that there are opportunities out there for people like me who don't have the highest GPA, and who didn't fit the description of the typical big law associate.

After submitting my paperwork to form LTA, I did a quick Google search of legal tech start-ups and reached out to them. Within a week, I had received over a dozen responses from start-ups that specialized in practice areas ranging from family law to cannabis compliance. A few back-and-forth emails later, I finally had a list of five companies (including Professor Moini's Documate) and seven attorneys and founders who were willing to speak at Gould.

I reserved Ackerman courtroom in the law building for the panel. The courtroom was typically used for moot court competitions, lectures, and other special events. The interior was designed to replicate an actual court of law, complete with a judge's bench and podium. The walls were wood-paneled and on the center of the wall behind the judge's bench was a seal emblazoned with a bald eagle that read "U.S. District Court—Central District of California." Everything about the room just seemed to bolster the gravitas of the speakers within.

Finally, the day of the panel came. It was a roaring success. The turnout was amazing, as the room was packed with students of all levels: JD candidates (1Ls, 2Ls, 3Ls) and LLMs. Some of my friends also showed up to provide moral support.

Even the director of Gould's experiential learning office came to speak with the founders about potentially setting up legal externship opportunities at their companies.

The panelists were from some pretty diverse backgrounds to say the least, but they all seemed to chime in with perfectly coordinated responses—almost like a chorus. Almost all of them had worked in big law for a few years before transitioning into the start-up scene; they all found gaps in the market that they were passionate about filling, and they all had a prodigious sense of resilience—a growth mindset that Angela harped on so fervently in her podcast. It was clear from the get-go that they were all cut from the same cloth.[22]

"*This is it,*" I thought to myself as I mediated the panel. "*This is the group of like-minded people that Professor Moini told me to network with.*" After the panel, I asked one of the speakers who especially stood out to me, Adam Kerpelman, if I could interview him for my book. Adam was the co-founder of Juris, an automated legal assistant that helps customers get illegally withheld security deposits back from their landlords.[23] Their website description: "Get Juris, and handle legal problems without a lawyer. Our automated assistant is fast, affordable, and all online. It empowers you to enforce your legal rights. No lawyer necessary. 5 minutes can recover you $1,500+."

He was wearing a grey blazer over a NASA T-shirt and brown khakis. I could tell by his demeanor and by the way he discussed the importance of having a growth mindset

---

22   Dragan Sutevski, "How to find the gap in an established market," Entrepreneurship in a box (blog), accessed September 3, 2020.

23   "Defend your rights. Fight for change," Juris, accessed September 3, 2020.

during the panel, which he referred to as having a "builder's mentality," that he would have some really valuable advice. So, I scheduled a phone call with Adam and interviewed him a week later.

I called Adam in the morning. He picked up on the first ring. We briefly greeted each other, and I began the interview. His tone was bright, as though he hadn't lost an ounce of energy since the panel. Starting off with some questions about his background to get a better context of the type of person Adam was, I asked him about what his law school experience was like. He told me he attended the University of Virginia (UVA) as an undergraduate and ended up coming to Los Angeles for law school. "So, I went to undergrad at UVA and then went to Southwestern Law School as part of their entertainment program. At the time, I wanted to go into entertainment law and maybe become an agent." For some reason, that made complete and total sense to me.

The reason Adam stood out from the other start-up founders was that he really knew how to grasp an audience's attention. The way he spoke was really dynamic and expressive. Unlike some of the other founders I met, he never delved too deeply into the technical details of his start-up, probably because he was cautious not to bore his listeners with minutiae. Adam had a natural warmth and charisma, which was exactly what I would imagine someone in the entertainment industry would be like.

I asked him to elaborate on what got him interested in legal technology, given his background in entertainment. "So, I finished college in 2005 at the University of Virginia and came to Los Angeles for film school. Our chief product officer (Juris's main programmer) got his Master of Fine Arts from the University of Southern California in interactive game production, and we worked together for a while and started a production company. That went on for about six years, and because production intersected with everything digital, I guess I just developed a strong interest in technology over time."

What Adam said hit what Professor Moini told me right on the nose. Getting out there and networking with people with diverse skill sets works, and Adam is living proof of that. But that didn't necessarily result in success right away. "Well actually, I did take a swing at another start-up idea in the health care space. But that idea ultimately didn't take off, I think, because I didn't have the expertise in health care that was necessary to really be successful in that space. Like, you really had to know the granule-level stuff about the industry—like a lobbyist. For me, I was like, 'I know a lot of doctors!' and that's why I thought it would work, but that just didn't cut it."

Adam explained that the service he initially tried to make was very similar to what Talkspace is today—except it was five years too soon. The idea was to connect patients with therapists to make counseling more efficient and accessible, while also remaining anonymous. He explained, "There's a gradient between 'Hey, I want to talk with somebody' and 'I need to go to treatment,' and we were really trying to get both of those types of patients to use the app. At the time, I had no idea what Talkspace was, so I did a quick internet search and found a description." Basically, Talkspace was an application that connects the user with a licensed therapist, who they can video chat, text, and send pictures to in a private chat room. The main aspect that made Talkspace special was its convenience—the application allowed people to get the help they needed without traveling to a brick-and-mortar office for care.

Adam continued, "Yeah, so at the time the law wasn't particularly favorable for telemedicine stuff. We had a lot of companies who were super interested, but ultimately their legal departments would spike the deal because they were worried that connecting with therapists across state lines would be violating state law. Ultimately, I don't think I could have executed a Talkspace-esque app at that age or with the understanding of the industry that I had, and I think that's why it didn't work out."

This was some really interesting insight. Adam's problem was a completely different one compared to Professor Moini's. In his case, it wasn't an issue of not having enough consumer interest or the sustainability of the business. Instead, it was an issue of timing. The law simply did not support telemedicine at the time and that scared people. Adam's story also highlighted another important point—no matter what type of legal tech start-up you're trying to create, knowing the law of the industry you're trying to break into is crucial.

I recalled Adam mentioning the importance of having a "builder's mindset" back at the panel, so I asked if he could explain what he meant and how it helped him overcome the obstacles in his life. He said, "I've always been a self-starter. As a kid, I used to start businesses on my own. For example,

I grew up in Baltimore, Maryland, and started my own photography company. I would attend a ton of sports games, mostly lacrosse games, and take pictures of the players and sell them to a lot of the preppy parents. And then when I was sixteen, I took a break from photography to become a professional swimmer. I started swimming full time and ended up going to University of Virginia (UVA), which is D1 top ten in swimming and went to the Olympic trials in 2004. So, my concept for what I would describe as a 'builder's mindset' or 'growth mindset' is basically seeing something intriguing and going, 'Okay, I have a plan. It's going to be really hard, but I'm gonna grind every day and get what I want.' It's like being on a sports team—it's just you every day against the clock—that's why a lot of swimmers are great entrepreneurs."

At this point I was pretty astounded. This was a guy who basically had been an entrepreneur his whole life. He went from selling photos as a kid, to becoming a professional D1 athlete, to going to film school; and now he's the founder of a legal tech start-up. Adam's story struck a chord with me. He's someone who, while not explicitly knowing where his path would lead, simply kept pushing forward by throwing himself into exciting projects.

It was amazing that Adam had done so much without burning out. It seemed too good to be true, so I asked him how he was able to avoid getting tired. It turned out he didn't.

He elaborated, "I think, in response to the latter part of your question, I did experience periods of discouragement. In fact, I think my builder's mindset, at some moments, took its toll on my mental health. The lesson I took away from my mental health journey is that when you have a project that you're excited about, you can't pour your whole life into it or it'll destroy your life emotionally, physically, and mentally. So, for example, when I was running the production company, I wasn't taking any personal time to myself. I was just hacking away trying to get into the digital space, make movies and commercials, and grow in size—and that just wrecked me. When we shut down and just stuck with making websites—I moved back to the East Coast, and I did client gigs, like building law firm websites for fifteen grand. At that point, I stopped on the creative side." He sighed over the phone. I could tell it was a dark time in his life. But then he chuckled and added, "My co-founders also got burnt out. We were there like 'GaryVee, it's not working!'"

Adam was referring to Gary Vaynerchuk (GaryVee for short), an American entrepreneur and motivational speaker. He's also the CEO and co-founder of VaynerMedia, a full-service digital agency that services Fortune 500 clients. His most famous piece of advice for entrepreneurs, which Adam was referencing, is to basically never stop working and to not expect success right away. Apparently, Adam and his team had taken that to an extreme.

Toward the end of our conversation, Adam ended with an important piece of advice. He explained, "It's easy in the start-up culture to conflate tenacity with a type of persistence that's not productive. Like, when you're working eighteen hours a day, there are diminishing returns, and it's just not worthwhile in the end. I think this also shows up in law firm culture, and I think that's why a lot of law firms are having conversations about mental health now. On some level, it's a work-life balance."

My conversation with Adam gave me a ton of great insight, but there were three main takeaways:

1. **Don't expect to succeed right off the bat**—it was good to be ambitious and start new projects, but it was clear from Adam's story that the first idea that I executed wasn't going to be my best. And I had to be okay with that.
2. **Establish a work-life balance that works for you**—no matter how hardworking, talented, or determined I became, there was only so much I could take before I burned out. I had to prioritize my mental health.
3. **Go out there and build something**—I just had to get out there and cut my teeth on something that really captured my interest.

I recalled Professor Moini had mentioned in her previous class that there was a hackathon happening in Los Angeles she encouraged everyone to participate in. It was still a couple weeks away, but after speaking with Adam, I knew this was my chance to start building.

CHAPTER 6

AMERICANAH

―――――

"This is what I like to call 'the danger of the single story,'" she said eloquently.[24] The words seamlessly fell from her mouth and echoed throughout the auditorium. She spoke about how as a child, she grew up in a conventional, middle-class Nigerian family. As per the norm, her family hired a live-in house boy, Fide, whom she knew nothing about aside from the fact that he was poor. One day she was shocked when she saw a beautiful basket Fide's brother had made. Explaining her surprise, she said, "All I had heard about [Fide's family] was how poor they were, so that it had become impossible for me to see them as anything else but poor. Their poverty was my single story for them."[25] Years later, when she left Nigeria to attend university in the United States, her American roommate reacted to her with similar shock when she discovered how perfect her English was, "She asked where I had learned to speak English so well and was confused when I said that Nigeria happened to have English as its official language. She asked if she could listen to what she called my

―――――

24 *TED*, "The danger of a single story | Chimamanda Ngozi Adichie," October 7, 2009, video, 19:16.
25 Ibid.

'tribal music,' and was consequently very disappointed when I produced my tape of Mariah Carey."[26]

I smiled in amusement at her response when I felt a tap on my shoulder. I took off my headphones and turned to my left to see who had interrupted me. "Jesse, can you watch that later? I know she's a good author, but we're in the middle of a meeting right now," Chinelo said sternly. Not realizing how absorbing the video would be, I had completely lost track of time. I turned to the front of the room and shuddered in embarrassment as I saw the rest of my classmates looking at me in annoyance. "Sorry," I apologized softly, sheepishly shoving my phone into my pocket as the video continued playing.

It was noon on the Tuesday following the tech panel and time for our weekly Student Bar Association (SBA) meeting. The girl who tapped me on the shoulder was my classmate, Chinelo. She wore a black blazer, long chain link earrings, and a silver nose ring. Her aesthetic was the perfect mix of edgy and professional. She also happened to be the person who had recommended I watch the particular *TED* Talk that caused my distraction by one of her favorite authors, Chimamanda Ngozi Adichie.

Chinelo and I didn't have much contact with one another during our first year of law school, since we were in different Super Sections, but eventually got to know each other better through SBA. We bonded quickly through our shared taste in music, particularly our mutual admiration for the Harlem-based rap artist Azealia Banks. But more importantly, it was

---

26 Ibid.

our similar experiences as first generation Americans with immigrant parents that drew us together.

Chinelo told me that Chimamanda's work really spoke to her because much of her literature encapsulated the struggles and sacrifices often overlooked when people talked about immigrants' pursuit of the enigmatic "American dream." Having never been exposed to African literature, I found Chinelo's book recommendations and cultural perspective very enlightening. And, as the semester progressed, I learned a great deal about her that both surprised and inspired me.

Growing up in a Catholic Nigerian-American household, Chinelo cultivated a strong work ethic at an early age, which led her to excel academically. She told me, "When I was young, I wasn't a genius, but I was definitely very smart for my age. I took math classes above my grade level and was even recommended to skip a grade. But my parents turned that down because they wanted me to have a regular life. People would compliment me a lot and tell me I was gifted, though, and that made me feel really good." The external gratification Chinelo received from the adults in her life instilled in her a need to be—and feel—perfect. Inevitably, that work ethic and the high standards Chinelo's parents set for her came with some baggage. She explained, "I think Nigerian parents, and immigrant parents in general, always tell us things like 'We came to this country for you,' and so they're really insistent that you do well because they basically gave away their culture and identities from their home country for you." That pressure and guilt about her parents' sacrifices pushed Chinelo early on to strive for perfection. And in the beginning, it worked.

Chinelo's strong academic record landed her at the University of California, Santa Barbara (UCSB) for her undergraduate studies where she majored in philosophy and political science, with an emphasis in international relations. It was during her time at UCSB when Chinelo first began really identifying with and celebrating her African heritage. She explained. "So, during my third year, I was really disappointed in the poli-sci department because I wanted to take a class on Africa and nation states in Africa, and the teachers were like, 'No, we don't have that here.' And I was like, how can you be a poli-sci department if you don't talk about Africa and only talk about Asia and Europe?" So, Chinelo took matters into her own hands and started a successful music show through her campus radio network KCSB 91.9 FM. Each week, she'd meet up with a group of friends at a studio under UCSB's Stork Towers and play African music.

Flying high both academically and socially through her radio show, Chinelo had jumped from strength to strength during her time at UCSB. And during her fourth year, it was time for Chinelo to capitalize on those successes as she began applying to law school. She explained how she was originally interested in becoming an immigration lawyer: "So, I'd always had this interest in doing public interest. Like, originally, I applied thinking I was going to do immigration law since my parents were immigrants. And, also, I think, in a more abstract sense, I wanted to go to law school to help people." Chinelo ultimately ended up accepting an offer to attend USC, given its competitive law school ranking and the generous scholarship she received. She was also confident she could tackle law school just like she had tackled all the other obstacles she had faced before—with verve and determination. However, law school proved to be a completely different animal.

Being in such a new environment for the first time in four years and having come straight from UCSB, Chinelo was eager to prove herself. On the first day of class, she hit the ground running. She explained, "From day one, I would take the most detailed notes because I needed that gratification. Like, I had gunner energy." Chinelo would spend endless hours going over and refining her notes and obsessing over making sure she was answering the professor's question with granular detail. The all-too-familiar pressure from her parents lit a flame inside Chinelo as she relentlessly pushed herself through the fall semester. She was confident her efforts would pay off, as they always had ever since she was a little girl.

The spirit of perfectionism hissed and gnarled at the pit of her stomach, spewing flamethrowers as it thrashed about. Like a skilled snake charmer, Chinelo, with years of experience and training, channeled those flames into her coursework. She scorched through civil procedure, property, and contract law. When finals came around, she spotted the legal issues on paper like a sniper, responding to each question with the detail, dexterity, and poise only someone who had spent a lifetime striving for perfection could possess.

Then, a few weeks later, the grades came out. And that fiery spirit immediately extinguished into ashes.

"I kinda realized that…being a gunner low-key didn't necessarily translate to good grades. So, I was the loudest person in the room and looked like I knew all the material…and my grades did not reflect that at all. So, really, I was out here looking stupid," she explained, placing a comical emphasis on the word "stupid." Chinelo had performed far below what she had expected of herself. And for the first time in her life, her cerebral gifts seemed to have failed her. All those glowing reports from grade school, her achievements at UCSB, and compliments about how smart she was from strangers seemed to melt away into the background.

It was as though Chinelo's "single story" had been shred to pieces. The story that she had heard throughout her entire childhood—that she was a smart girl. The perfect girl, who worked hard and fought to improve herself with all her might. Every time she focused on a goal, whether it was getting perfect grades, praise from her elders, or acceptance into her dream school, she attained it. But her first semester law school grades fell dramatically outside the scope of the narrative Chinelo had come to identify with. It was like the basket Fide's brother had made or the Mariah Carey tape that Chimamanda's roommate had expected to be "tribal music." Those first semester grades flew in the face of every compliment Chinelo had received growing up. And it left her absolutely shell-shocked.

Piling on top of the weight of her grades were the words of the career counselors who told Chinelo she wasn't competitive enough for big law jobs or the summer associate positions she was interested in. Taking one speedy glance at her transcripts, her advisors surmised that Chinelo just didn't have it in her to get into the top programs.

In one fell swoop, another "single story" had completely overwritten her original one. And in this new version, there was no possibility for someone like Chinelo to obtain a high paying job straight out of law school, no possibility of competing with individuals who were ranked higher than she was in the class, and no possibility of her being considered for a position at one of the upper-echelon law firms recruiting through OCI. This new story crushed her. "I'm lucky I didn't drop out," she said, recalling the difficult months following the release of our fall semester grades.

Chinelo was, in fact, very lucky she didn't drop out of law school. Though it affected her emotionally, the new "single story" that career services had written for Chinelo ultimately didn't accurately predict what would happen next. Having applied to a competitive summer program prior to the release of fall grades, Chinelo interviewed for and ultimately accepted an offer to work at the U.S. Securities and Exchange Commission (SEC) honors program during the summer after her first year.

Working at the SEC gave her a strong competitive advantage going into OCI. Reflecting on the significance of the program, she explained to me, "The thing that made working at the SEC so great was that a lot of big firms go against the SEC in litigation, and so those firms want to hire people who've worked for the SEC in the past to get that insider experience."

Chinelo's time working for the SEC completely rebooted her outlook on law school. She told me, "I would ask the SEC people, 'I didn't do well my first year. Should I still go through with OCI, like is it worth it?' And they all resoundingly said yes." Not only did they encourage her, Chinelo's coworkers advised her to bid for as many firms as she could, except for the highest ranked firms that were completely out of her reach.

One attorney at the SEC told her that he had a lower GPA and went to a worse law school than USC and still got a firm offer. He told her emphatically that there was absolutely no reason Chinelo shouldn't shoot her shot. So, when OCI came around, Chinelo marched into the USC Hotel for her interviews with renewed confidence.

When she walked into the rooms to greet her prospective employers, Chinelo realized she had no reason to doubt herself so much. She was more qualified than she thought and was determined to come out of the experience with no regrets. Most importantly, Chinelo was determined to tune out the individual "single stories" she had heard about herself. She realized in that moment that what each person thought about her—whether it was that she was smart, stupid, or uncompetitive—didn't accurately define her.

She knew that, just as the "single story" of her being academically gifted her entire life couldn't predict her fall semester law school GPA, the "single story" the career counselors told her about being uncompetitive at OCI similarly couldn't predict whether she would walk out of her interviews with an offer. Once Chinelo finished her first round of screeners, she received several callbacks. And after a second round of interviews, she ended up receiving a firm offer, which she triumphantly accepted.

I thought about how Chinelo's experience tied back to what Chimamanda had explained in her lecture. Specifically, I noticed that the danger of Chinelo's "single story" lay in its one-sidedness. Stories invariably mattered. But individually, they were never dispositive of her success or the trajectory of her life. The "single story" of her childhood teachers and relatives telling Chinelo that she was smart was encouraging and empowering. It built up her confidence and led her to many wins. But it didn't capture the entire picture. It was like a polaroid with half the frame blurred out because the photographer had his thumb on the lens. The incomplete frame was precisely why receiving those fall semester grades was so jarring to Chinelo. By contrast, the "single story" the career counselors painted just by glancing at her transcript was discouraging, yet also incomplete and ultimately inaccurate. That story didn't consider the fact that Chinelo would be admitted to the SEC honors program and receive the guidance and insight from her coworkers.

In the end, the biggest lesson from Chinelo's experience was clear: no singular story about herself—good, bad, or indifferent—could accurately define her. Each "single story" Chinelo had heard by itself was faulty in some way. Only when the stories were woven together did they form an intricate and vibrant tapestry that accurately encapsulated her identity. She could still be the smart girl her middle school teachers always told her she was and still perform poorly in law school; she could also be uncompetitive at OCI and still receive an offer from a law firm.

I thought about how I could apply the lessons I had learned from Chimamanda and Chinelo to my own life. What was my "single story?" I suppose the sound bite I constantly heard throughout my childhood was that I was "almost" gifted or "almost" smart enough, but not quite there. By contrast, throughout college, I performed very well in many of my classes and graduated with high honors. I had to balance out these stories in my head, like Chinelo, and realize that, perhaps, the kid who failed to test into the gifted class six times in middle school could still be an intelligent and great lawyer. And perhaps, the honors student who graduated magna cum laude from Emory could also perform abysmally in his first year of law school, learn from his mistakes, and improve. Individually, each story missed the mark. Yet, together, they demonstrated that I was a multifaceted human being. And by realizing this, I could repair—at least to a small extent—my sense of dignity and self-respect.

After the SBA meeting ended, I pulled out my phone to finish watching Chimamanda's *TED* Talk. Still standing at the white podium, she concluded with one last takeaway: "I would like to end with this thought: that when we reject the single story, when we realize that there is never a single story about any place, we regain a kind of paradise."[27] The room erupted in applause, and the screen faded to black.

---

27 Ibid.

CHAPTER 7

MARTY

———

"I'm really interested in technology, especially in the context of health care," I croaked.

I paused for a moment. I was overcaffeinated, and my thoughts were spiraling inside my head at montage speed. It was like I was face-to-face with a swirling vortex of colors, trying to fish out the most vibrant ones, but they kept slipping from my grasp.

"I guess because…," I began before trailing off.

She started typing.

"Well, I definitely believe in efficiency, and I think with the rise of telehealth and virtual therapy, technology is certainly on its way to reshaping the industry," I said with an exhale.

She smiled and nodded.

I was at the One Medical headquarters at the Two Embarcadero Center Office in San Francisco. About a week after the legal tech panel, I got a call back from a recruiter for their summer legal associate position. I had been at the office since 2 p.m. and spoken to three members of the team back-to-back. It was almost 5 p.m. My body was exhausted, but my mind was shooting fireworks.

After the interviews concluded, I thanked the last team member for their time and left. I knew I had stumbled a couple times throughout, mostly due to nerves, but overall, I thought I did fairly well. My passion leapt out of me, as I spoke about founding Gould's Legal Technology Association and my intent to participate in a hackathon in March. The only thing was, I still didn't know exactly what I was going to pitch at the hackathon, so my responses were a bit vague.

Since One Medical was a health tech start-up that combined primary care with telemedicine (i.e. the remote diagnosis and treatment of patients using telecommunications technology), I told them my idea was for a mental health app specifically geared toward law firms and practicing attorneys, and they seemed impressed by that.[28] The job description highlighted that One Medical was looking for an entrepreneurial self-starter, so I knew from the beginning this was the perfect match for me.

I was enamored by everything I saw and touched—the tall, narrow staircases of the office that represented the efficiency and space-saving qualities of the city, the friendly and casually dressed professionals who didn't obsess over their appearances because they were too engaged in their work,

---

28   "About One Medical," One Medical, accessed September 10, 2020.

and the elegant glass walls of the workspaces that provided just enough privacy to be productive while still feeling connected with the rest of the office.

I was in love with San Francisco, and I was in love with One Medical. I wanted to write my wedding vows to the city and sing "Honey" by Mariah Carey as loudly and as off-key as possible in front of everyone, so I could express how committed I was to moving there. After exiting the office and heading down the escalator of the building, a warm breeze greeted me at the entryway. The Embarcadero. It's the eastern waterfront and roadway off the Port of San Francisco, along the bay.

The last time I was in San Francisco was back in 2016, while I was in the B.B.A. program at Goizueta Business School. I went on a "tech trek" for business students looking to work for start-ups in the bay area, and I distinctly recalled feeling absolutely entranced by the view of the bay and walking alongside the trolley tracks, dreaming of someday working in San Francisco.

The city was exactly as I remembered it. Busy. Innovative. Tall. I mentioned to my interviewer earlier that I loved how everything in San Francisco was "vertical." It wasn't like Los Angeles, where buildings were spread out and commutes took forever. No, SF was different. You could walk from the Google office to One Medical in twenty minutes, and there were so many booming start-ups in between. I was in a small, bustling microcosm of inventors, entrepreneurs, and tech-savvy workers, who epitomized the "builder's mindset." It seemed like everyone was multitasking; joggers chatted with clients through their earpieces, people in suits were stuffing their faces with sandwiches while responding to questions between every bite, and I was on my way back from an interview at an incredible health care start-up. I felt invincible. I was crushing it!

I made my way back to the apartment where my childhood friend Marty lived. He let me crash at his place for the weekend. Marty was a technical writer for Google and had started working at the headquarters about four months prior to my trip to SF. He went to college in Florida, where he double majored in computer science and economics.

In addition to technical writing, Marty was also an avid creative writer and ran his own site, fakeandbasic.com, where he posted fictional stories, career updates, and views on gender identity.[29] He always had a sui generis nature: outspoken and unapologetic, especially during high school. Except, back then, "he" was actually "she." The Marty I knew when we attended The Shipley School together went by "Mimi." We were the only two Chinese American students in our class of about eighty, and we bonded pretty quickly as a result.

Fast forward six years and I was sitting in the living room of Marty's apartment. On the table—a box of half-eaten chocolate chip cookies that Marty had packed from the dining hall at Google.

"I get free meals there every day. Their cookies are my favorite," he said as he sat down at the kitchen table.

---

29 "Infrequently Asked Questions," Fake and Basic, accessed September 10, 2020.

He pulled out his laptop and began reading through his emails.

"This is so surreal," I said aloud.

"I mean, who would've thought all these years later we'd meet up again in San Francisco of all places," I observed.

"Yeah," he replied.

He was reading something intently on his screen. I smiled and shook my head in awe. It was as though I was in a weird fantasy that sixteen-year old me dreamt up in his sleep. I stared at the mirror across from me in the living room and saw both of our reflections. I was still dressed in my interview clothes. One Medical had told me to wear "start-up attire," which I thought meant a suit minus the jacket. I definitely looked tired, but overall, I was feeling the look. Marty was wearing a red floral dress, a pink fur coat, and sandals—a complete contradiction to his authoritarian, no-bullshit personality.

Eight years ago, in 2012, Marty transferred from Baldwin, an all-girls private school in Bryn Mawr, Pennsylvania, to Shipley, a small coeducational private school just across the street where I was just beginning my junior year. Even then, Marty told me that everything about his aesthetic was meant to "troll" people. Even though he identified as a girl at the time and dressed in the most effeminate manner possible, deep down he was "masculine-centre." In other words, he always thought of himself as and believed he was, in his essence, a boy.

Weeks later in a text he explained to me, "I liked messing with people; I noticed culturally everyone who dressed girly was a specific stereotype of this helpless prissy girly girl, and I just wanted to completely shatter that stereotype by being completely brash, uncouth, and loquacious as fuck. I didn't care about grades or status at the time—I just wanted to be a rebel." But this attitude changed sometime during his senior year of high school. He mentioned pressure from his mother and other personal stressors in his life at the time caused him to get his act together, and by the time he was a freshman at New College of Florida, Marty was a workaholic.

Still, the difference I noticed in Marty wasn't just that he now took his life seriously and was committed to his work. It was more than that—he was also far calmer, more collected, and logical in both his thoughts and actions. Gone were the days he would sneer at me in the back of the bus, yelling crude sexual jokes much to the chagrin of his sister and me.

"Marty, you're just different now," I blurted out.

He raised an eyebrow without looking up from the screen.

"No—I mean in a good way," I quickly corrected myself. I added, "Like—I just feel a sense of maturity from you now."

He smirked.

"Yeah, I kinda got rid of parts of myself that people didn't like and became committed to this image of me that people had in their minds. I think that helped me a lot socially."

He took a sip of tea and sighed before adding, "I kinda also hated myself too though because it was like, 'Oh wow, the real you is actually really defective, and you have to put on this fake persona for people to like you.'"

"Oh. I see," I said quietly.

Suddenly, my saccharine elation tasted a bit sour in my mouth. There were sacrifices we had to make to be successful, and Marty was no exception. Despite how loud, obnoxious, and crude his past behavior was, that was his personality. It was who he was...or at least, it was who Mimi was. Of course, there was nothing wrong with adding a bit more polish to your character to be a bit more "work appropriate," but it still saddened me to know he had to dampen his spirit.

"Did you always want to come to San Francisco?" I said hesitantly, trying to change the subject.

"Yeah," he said nonchalantly. "Pretty much."

Marty was a computer science student and everyone in his major would talk about Silicon Valley like it was some kind of "golden dream." I guess to them, it was their ultimate concern in life. After Marty's third year in college, he landed a lucrative internship as an iOS engineer at Urban Outfitters in Philadelphia and decided that summer he would try his best to get to the bay area. During his fourth and final year of college, Marty relentlessly prepared for interviews, wrote articles, and sharpened his technical knowledge and skills. He went to hackathons every weekend and did, as he described, a "shit-ton" of networking.

And by the time he graduated, he got a job right away at a start-up in San Francisco.

"Wait. Did you take a break after graduation?"

"Nope," he said reflexively.

It was clearly a tender moment etched in his memory. Marty had packed his bags right after graduation and was on a flight to San Francisco the very next day, with little to no time to say goodbye to the friends he had made the past four years.

"Things got bad pretty much right away," he said as he typed rigorously on his laptop without even looking up.

He added, "I originally wanted to take the summer off after senior year just to relax, but they told me I had to start working right away, and if I didn't, they would rescind my offer. That was the first red flag."

The next year for Marty was a distorted nightmare of what he had imagined Silicon Valley would be—like pouring the contents of a dream in a blender and watching it swirl into a vortex of hell. Marty was already completely burnt out from networking and interviewing for jobs. Yet, he still had to put in twelve-hour days every day of the week, including weekends. As a new graduate, Marty had a comparably lower skill level than his associates when it came to coding and needed time and mentorship to grow and learn. However, all the engineers were too busy putting out "fires" that would constantly pop up.

Marty described a typical "fire" would be like an investor suddenly wanting a new feature on an application the start-up was developing within weeks, when usually such a feature would take years. Everyone was working weekends and the leadership did not care at all about the employees' well-being.

"They only cared about results. It didn't matter how hard I worked or how much time I put into my assignments. If I didn't attain the endgame, I wasn't just chastised—I was deemed incompetent." In the end Marty got fired. And for the next six months, he fell into a deep depression.

"I basically went through an existential crisis. Like, the whole time in college, my self-worth was built upon my status and productivity. And, without that, I just felt worthless." He shook his head and chuckled. "Man, that was a shitty time."

He told me about how for months after he was fired, he would just lie in bed all day with terrible suicidal thoughts. For him, there was just no point in living if he couldn't have the golden life he had always dreamed about. The once passionate, hard-working, and driven Marty from college had deteriorated into a depressed blob.

As Marty told this part of his story, I felt gutted for him. To have a dream in the palm of your hand and have it snatched from you and crushed into a million pieces would make anyone cry. But the thing was, I knew Marty. Obviously in retrospect I knew this wasn't the end of the story given that he was currently working at Google, but even had I not seen his eventual success, the Marty I knew back then was an unapologetic rebel. And despite grooming out some of the cruder split-ends of his personality, the inner subversive Marty I had always known was still alive and kicking.

"Yeah, so basically I was like fuck this shit," he continued without skipping a beat. I smiled. "This whole time, even in college, I had this blog that I really enjoyed as a hobby but didn't take seriously. So, one day, I decided to pick up writing again and used it as a coping mechanism. I realized that whenever I wrote, I felt less bad about myself because it was something I was good at." That's right. I almost forgot; Marty was always great at English. While I had tested into all of the advanced-level math and science courses at Shipley, while missing out on the humanities honors courses, Marty consistently placed in honors English and used to proofread my essays in the library before class. Completely ironic that I ended up in law school, and he ended up at Google.

"I thought to myself, it doesn't really matter how much I work or how productive I am—these start-up people don't care. They treated me like a machine and tossed me out when I couldn't churn out the product they wanted. So, I figured, let me just do something that I actually care about." Marty already had a technical background from college and, utilizing his writing skills, began writing technical content on his site. After a while, his content started gaining traction on the internet.

One day, an acquaintance of Marty's who was already working at Google forwarded one of his blog posts to a recruiter, who then reached out via email to interview him. They were specifically looking for a technical writer and, after interviewing Marty, extended an offer. "And I've been working there ever since," he said as he got up to wash his mug.

What Marty described was basically a complete overhaul of his values and beliefs. He grew from an image of self-worth rooted in status and success to one centered upon his art and creative writing, using his site as an outlet.

"Are you angry at all? Resentful at the people in the past who treated you poorly?" I asked. "Not really. I'm not angry about the start-up, but I'm resentful of the tech industry overall," he replied nonchalantly. He explained how despite finding success and landing his job at Google through his writing, he still garners odd reactions when he mentions his writing. According to Marty, people in the tech industry simply didn't value art or creative projects as much. But they'd quickly change their attitudes toward the subject in conversation once he mentions he works at Google. "I guess the way I 'showed them' was by being myself," he added. "I just figured out my own path on my own through my creativity and being true to myself—which includes all aspects of me, my gender identity, and personality."

Everyone had counted Marty out before. His own mother thought he was a complete failure in high school. And for a long time, he had a chip on his shoulder because of it. "I will say this—I think having an 'I'll show you' mentality definitely helped me with my career and getting me to where I wanted to go, but I definitely don't think it's sustainable in the long run. It caused me a lot of pain and completely burned me out. And when I see people who have something to prove, I sense this desperate energy emanating from them that makes me sad because I know how toxic and painful that feeling can be. My biggest advice, as trite as it sounds: Be you."

It was midnight. "Ah, I better go to sleep. I gotta be up early to go to the Mountain View office tomorrow. Good night." He turned off the light and walked down the hallway, his footsteps pattering into the distance until they were inaudible.

I turned to my side as the streetlight outside shined through a crack in the curtain above me. I thought intently about everything I had learned in just the last twenty-four hours. Marty really had been through hell and back and finally made it because he did two things. The first was he identified what made him happy—writing—and focused not on how it could further his career but on how it made him feel. It made him feel whole, and it made him feel valued. Not valued in the sense that other people respected him more, but rather a sense of value that came from within—it allowed him to positively reassess his worth without considering external validation. What other people thought just didn't matter at the time; all that mattered was being able to get out of bed and putting one foot in front of the other until he felt better.

The second thing Marty did, after exhausting his "I'll show you" mentality, was let go. He let go of the stinging pain of rejection when his start-up threw him out like a piece of garbage. He let go of his mother's belief that he was a complete failure in high school. Most importantly, he let go of the golden life he felt he needed to realize in order to be whole.

My eyelids drooped and within a few minutes I was fast asleep. As I entered REM sleep, my mind began dreaming up bright, swirling colors until suddenly I was standing in the middle of The Embarcadero. Everything was golden, from the people jogging down the street to my own hands and feet. My face split into a wide smile. "Home," I said aloud. "I'm home."

CHAPTER 8

MENTALBRIEF PART 1

———

I flagged down my Uber at the side of the road next to my apartment and got in the vehicle. I was on my way to Documate headquarters in Culver City, where the Global Legal Hackathon was taking place.[30] A couple weeks after returning from my trip to San Francisco, Professor Moini announced that she had decided to host the competition at the Documate office this year.

The 2020 Global Legal Hackathon was an international competition, where thousands of participants formed teams, pitched ideas, and created technology-based legal solutions.[31] Overall, there were three rounds. The first round took place at basically every major city in the US, so the closest location for me was in Culver City. Each participating city had one winning team, which would then move on to the second round done as a virtual pitch to a judging panel. Finally, at the third round, finalists would be flown out to London, UK, to present their solutions in front of a live audience.[32]

———

30 "Global Legal Hackathon: World's Largest Legal Hackathon," Global Legal Hackathon, accessed September 3, 2020.

31 Ibid.

32 Ibid.

I was absolutely stoked about pitching something at the regional level. The problem was, I didn't really have a clear idea of what I was going to pitch. I thought long and hard about what had brought me this far to begin with. By the time the weekend came around, nothing came to mind. Still, I was determined to give it my all and see where my experience would take me.

It took about half an hour to get from USC to the headquarters, and when I arrived the sun had already begun setting. The first night was just a formality, so I wasn't expecting too much excitement. Participants were supposed to just come in, introduce each other, and form teams before the competition officially started the next morning. I passed through the tall glass doors and asked the doorman to let me up to the tenth floor, where Professor Moini's office was. As I walked past the lobby, I noticed everything, from the plush couches to the chrome coffee tables, was so sleek and modern. I exited to the tenth floor and entered another lobby area where a group of people were sitting at a wooden table chatting with each other.

"Hey Jesse, what's up!" I heard from a familiar voice. It was Arsh, a classmate of mine from Legal Innovations Lab. "Oh hey, Arsh! How's it going?" I replied cheerfully. I was still in a pretty good mood from my One Medical interview and was excited to cut my teeth on a new project. "Pretty good, I was just about to share my idea for the hackathon with some of the developers here to see if they were interested in joining my team," he said with a smile. Arsh was no stranger to the start-up space. He's executed start-ups and pitched ideas to angel investors before, so I had no doubt he had come fully prepared. I sat down across from him and listened intently, as he explained his pitch.

His idea arose from the context of the coronavirus (COVID-19) pandemic, which, little did we know at the time, would rapidly evolve into a national emergency within the next two weeks following the competition. He explained how a lot of people don't have access to lawyers because they simply can't afford them and, after interviewing multiple prospective clients, he discovered that most of them just went online and read stuff from blogs and other public websites. Some resorted to LegalZoom, an online platform that helps customers make legal documents for a small fee. To them, these were the only affordable resources they could obtain.

He began explaining his idea energetically: "The thing is, when you're filling out forms—if you fill out the wrong part of the form or if you fill it out the wrong way, it's just not functional. And, so, what I thought of was an online, public teaching platform for laypeople who've had little to no legal experience to learn about the law and solve their own legal issues. In essence, it's a Khan Academy for the law, and it's called 'Co-Counsel.'"[33] Khan Academy. I remember using it in high school back when it was just a YouTube channel where some guy posted videos of algebra tutorials. Since then, it's turned into a nonprofit that provides free online courses and lessons.

After he finished chatting with the developers, I was curious to learn more about Arsh and his background as a start-up founder. It was already past 9 p.m., and the office was almost empty. I figured I should leave too and come back early tomorrow morning for a fresh start and began to leave.

---

33 "For every student, every classroom. Real Results," Khan Academy, accessed September 10, 2020.

"Hey Jesse! Did you want to ask me something?" Arsh's voice echoed down the hallway of glass partitioned offices.

"Oh yeah, I did. I just figured it's getting kinda late and you're probably tired," I replied.

"Nonsense! I was just about to get set up for the night," he said energetically.

Arsh pulled out his laptop and draped his jacket over a chair as his screen turned on.

"Wait, you're staying?" I said surprised.

I knew Arsh was dedicated, but I had no idea he was willing to pull an all-nighter the first night of the hackathon after everyone else had already left.

"Yeah, I really want to get things going, and I'm pretty excited. Come sit. Ask away," he said brightly.

I pulled up a chair and took out my notebook.

When I mentioned earlier that this wasn't Arsh's first rodeo—that was an understatement. Turns out, back in November 2019, Arsh had already launched a start-up and an application into stores. The app was called "WellSayer"—a relationship management software to help users set goals with their relationships.[34]

---

34   "Transform your life with guided journaling," WellSayer, accessed September 10, 2020.

He explained: "Basically, the long-term vision, like our five-to ten-year goal, was to create a fundamental measure of human wellbeing. So, for example, you, 'Jesse,' could look at every aspect of your life from your housing condition, career, friendships, etc. and be able to quantify how much meaning that aspect brings to your life. Dollars don't capture the value of health, relationships, etc. We wanted to create a dataset to quantify the value of all human interactions. Scholars divide health into three categories—physical, mental, and social. So, WellSayer's aim was to focus on social health and keep track of users' connections with other people." So, in essence, it was a way for users to be able to assess which relationships they should be investing the most time in, depending on how much value the relationship brings to you.

"It sounds like it worked out then. That's a really interesting idea, I feel like a lot of people would be interested!" I said optimistically.

"Not exactly...," he replied in a lowered tone.

Arsh explained that WellSayer ultimately hit a dead end. Based on what users of the app were saying, most of them were using WellSayer to support transactional relationships, like building a robust professional network and trying to foster relationships that will help them get the "most bang from their buck" with their colleagues. Except, this didn't seem like a problem to me. I thought that so long as customers were interested in using the app and the app actually worked, then what's the problem? But it's actually more complicated than that.

He continued, "We had a clear vision for WellSayer that we—that is, my co-founder and I—really believed in. Most of the time, start-ups aren't worth it. Like, it's a bunch of work that's probably not gonna pay off, and it's probably not gonna help people that much. But people keep going because they believe in the mission. That's what, in my view, keeps the start-up alive." WellSayer was originally supposed to be an app that would increase people's quality of life and how they relate to others. But instead, the users were turning it into a money-making machine to boost their professional careers—which was the exact opposite of its intended purpose.

Arsh further explained that he predicted that down the road, the mostly likely scenario would be to sell his idea for Well-Sayer to LinkedIn for professional purposes and monetary gain, and that just wasn't in alignment with WellSayer's vision. Also, looking from a bird's eye-view of the relationship management application industry, most apps, within three to five years, either ceased to exist or became purely transactional. So, it was inevitable that WellSayer would result in one of those two outcomes.

"When I realized there wasn't a way forward, that's when I got really depressed. I mean, this was an app we had been working on for two and a half years. We did a lean start-up thing and built solutions and started scaling up. And all of that just seemed like it was for nothing," he explained. By early December 2019, Arsh felt like he had hit rock bottom. He lamented the fact that he could've spent the previous year volunteering for an organization or making a lot of money, but instead he "built something that helps no one and got nowhere."

"Can you tell me a bit about how you coped with your disappointment? Like, was there anything that helped mitigate the impact of what happened?" I asked.

"Yeah! Well, there were actually two things that helped me transition from that moment," he responded brightly.

After doing a bit of research, Arsh found out this basically happens with every start-up. For example, Slack used to be a gaming start-up before it became a communication start-up.[35] Change was a natural process in start-up culture and, at the time, that wasn't something that Arsh was thinking about.

Also, Arsh had really great support, which helped him a lot emotionally. "I had an amazing co-founder, Ben Douglas, who was an engineering major at University of Louisville where we both went to school. Just knowing that I wasn't alone at that moment of defeat was comforting." Ben also had an optimistic take on their circumstances. He reminded Arsh that they had learned a great deal from the experience and there was still a tiny percentage of users that were fostering social interactions, as opposed to transactional ones. There was still this diamond in the rough—that handful of people who actually care about relationships and were using WellSayer in ways that aligned with its mission. It was a small win, but a win, nonetheless.

"So, what now? How did you use that small win, or did you use it?" I asked.

---

35   "The Slack origin story: How a whimsical online game became an enterprise software giant," Tech Crunch, accessed September 10, 2020.

"Oh, we completely scrapped WellSayer," he replied with a smile.

He added, "I mean, we still have the app in stores, but we ended up transitioning into another space."

That space was journaling. At the start of 2020, after about a month of reconfiguring his game-plan, Arsh picked a different path and full-sail committed to it. His new app? A guided journal that allows users to reflect on parts of life. The journal prompts the user to unpack the experiences they've had in life thus far and potentially share those insights. Arsh explained that right now, there doesn't seem to be a structured platform on the market right now for collecting those insights, so the app could potentially be a big game-changer.

"We also talked to Anna Barber—the managing director of Techstars LA—about it and got some great feedback."[36] Techstars, as Arsh described, is like the University of California system of start-up universities. That is if there were universities for start-ups.[37] It's basically a ninety-day program that sets start-up founders up with world-class mentors.[38] The point is to help founders connect and build their businesses.

"We had this hour-long conversation about WellSayer and managing relationships, and her response…was kind of luke-warm," he explained. Arsh said his chat with Anna was a moment of authenticity and humility. She was being polite, but the final takeaway was that WellSayer just wasn't the

---

36   "dot.LA Dives In: Featuring Anna Barber, Managing Director of Tech-stars LA," dot.LA, accessed September 10, 2020.

37   Ibid.

38   Ibid.

greatest idea. Then, her tone changed when he brought up the journaling app idea. "When I discussed the second idea, she was really excited. I think that was one of the more concrete moments that really pushed us forward," he recalled.

I finished jotting everything down in my notebook and thanked Arsh for his time before ordering my Lyft back home. On my way back to my apartment, I thought deeply about the lessons I had gleaned from our conversation. Here was a guy who spent an entire year of his life committed to a project that ended up at a completely dead end. But there were two clear things in his life at the time that allowed Arsh to shift gears and recover from the setback more quickly than usual.

The first was his network. Arsh had, without knowing it, taken Professor Moini's advice and collaborated with a co-founder who was equally as committed, optimistic, and hard-working. Having a like-minded individual who was experiencing the same struggle as he was at the time helped to soften the blow of WellSayer's failure.

The second factor was Arsh's ability to recognize the silver lining through the small, seemingly insignificant wins that he scored throughout developing WellSayer. One small win was the fact that some users of the application were still using it in alignment with the app's original purpose. Another was the consumer insight they gained from WellSayer's active users. The insight gained from those users could be used in the future for Arsh's journaling app. Finally, perhaps the most minute win of them all was simply Anna Barber's reaction to the journaling app idea. Arsh was able to regain his excitement and inspiration he had for start-ups through a positive reaction to his idea.[39]

The driver pulled up to the curb outside my apartment. As I walked into the complex, fishing for the key fob in my pocket to get up the elevator, I thought about how I might apply Arsh's advice to my own project for the hackathon. Tomorrow was the first full day of the hackathon, and I couldn't wait to get started.

---

39   "The Power of Small Wins," *Harvard Business Review*, accessed September 10, 2020.

CHAPTER 9

MENTALBRIEF PART 2

My phone chimed. It was 9 a.m. My eyelids clung desperately to each other as I forced them apart. Somehow forgetting that technology does not respond to violence, I flung my arm out from underneath my blanket and shot it like a torpedo at my phone, knocking it forcefully off my nightstand. The alarm stopped. I might've broken it but was too tired to care. I rolled over in bed, trying to drift back to sleep. As I attempted to empty my brain of any thoughts or stressors, this sense of dread began sprouting in the pit of my stomach.

Something was off. Suddenly, I jolted awake. I forgot I had a phone call set up with my legal technology professor at ten! The previous week, I had asked Professor Rich if I could interview her for my book. It was still four hours until our call, but I hadn't even come up with the questions I'd ask because I had been so preoccupied with coming up with an idea for the hackathon.

I quickly made my way to the kitchen and brewed some coffee. The machine hummed beside me as I sat down and opened my laptop at the kitchen table. I reached into my book bag lying beside me in search of a black pen and spiral notebook.

Rummaging through the disorganized landfill of candy wrappers, loose-leaf papers, and breath mints lining the bottom of my bag, I felt around for something flat and something pointy. I felt the ballpoint pen poking the tip of my finger and, as I reached further down to grab it, it pierced my skin. I recoiled and bumped my arm into the table, causing a cascade of steaming black liquid to flood out of my mug and onto the surface of my laptop keyboard. Staring at the black contents spilled across the electronic device containing my entire life (i.e. my law school notes and outlines), I stood in absolute shock. Paralyzed.

For a moment, I could feel myself having an out-of-body experience, like Ebenezer Scrooge from *A Christmas Carol* when the ghosts of Christmas past, present, and future made him look at himself in an alternate reality to witness the repercussions of his miserliness. Floating above the kitchen cabinets, I looked down upon myself as my body stood perfectly still in the middle of my kitchen.

Then, violently clutching its chest, my body dramatically collapsed to the floor, convulsing a few times on the ground before becoming motionless. I grimaced at the sight of my corpse. Immediately, bright colors flashed before me at montage speed. I was being transported into another segment of this alternate reality sequence. When the colors disappeared, I found myself floating above a cemetery, with lush green hills and rows of grey, rounded stones lined with tiny American flags and daisies. I spotted a tombstone in the distance with my name on it. Floating closer, I squinted my eyes to make out the engraved text. I read the words aloud: "Here lies Jesse Wang...who died of stressing himself out too much.... We will remember him for all the times he complained about law school...and for not being able to finish it...because he died." I sighed loudly and screamed at the heavens above me.

Shaking my fist at the sky, I cursed at whatever ethereal forces were controlling this stress-induced astral projection in frustration, "Whoever you are, can you give me a break? Just take me back to my kitchen so I can fix my damn laptop!" "Jesse, get your shit together," a deep god-like voice boomed back curtly. The green lawn of the cemetery morphed back into the wood-paneled floor, as my brain began to regain consciousness.

Shaking my head vigorously, I snapped out of my trance-like state and found myself still standing in front of my laptop, which was surprisingly still on despite the liquid massacre that should have forced it into a vegetative state. I quickly ran to a nearby cupboard to get a roll of paper towels, cleaned up the mess, and turned my laptop off to dry.

I then proceeded to sit in the living room to digest what had just happened. My computer was dead, I didn't have an idea for the hackathon, I hadn't heard back from One Medical yet, and I was totally unprepared for my call. My mental health was running on empty and this was the final straw. No—it wasn't even a straw. It was like an entire haystack had fallen from the sky all at once that broke the proverbial camel's back. "I don't wanna die," I whispered to myself with tears in my eyes, "especially not when my tombstone's going to put me on blast like that." I whimpered pathetically as I curled up into a fetal position on my couch. I knew I was being such a baby. But I didn't care. My life felt like it was falling apart, and I just wanted to wallow for a bit.

Deep down I knew, though, that life would only get harder from here on out. I mean, this wasn't even the real world yet—this was law school. Was I really going to have a heart attack and die over spilled coffee? So many people—so many lawyers out there have faced far worse. But then again, when I became one of those lawyers having to face situations ten or twenty times more stressful than spilling coffee on my laptop, what would I do? How could I survive that level of strain on my health? What could I do in the meantime to help me fight through those tough moments?

Then, it hit me. There was one aspect of being a lawyer that had yet to be addressed, a gap in the market that I could fill—one that would benefit the most people within the legal field: mental health. But more specifically, the mental health of lawyers. I could pitch an app aimed to help lawyers cope with stress and improve their overall mental and emotional wellbeing. An app that would help cultivate mental grit and stamina, so that when lawyers fall into that dark pit of despair, they have the tools to climb out of it. In fact, this was perfect because lawyers are the most depressed group of professionals—a fact we were kindly reminded of several times during first week of orientation. In fact, one study by Johns Hopkins University found that lawyers as a group were nearly four times more likely to suffer from depression than the average person.[40] Frequently,

---

40 Andrea Ciobanu and Stephen M. Terrell, "Out of the Darkness: Overcoming Depression among Lawyers," *GPSolo, Vol. 32, No. 2, Healthcare* (Spring 2015): 36-39

this abysmal statistic has been cited as caused by the fact that lawyers tend to be emotionally withdrawn high achievers, perfectionists, and workaholics—all of which contribute to high stress and depression rates.[41]

I also remembered Professor Moini briefly mentioning in a previous class that she had worked with a partner at Sidley who had tragically committed suicide in 2018. I pulled out my phone and did a quick Google search. The first link that came up was an article titled "'Big Law Killed My Husband': An Open Letter from a Sidley Partner's Widow, the wife of Sidley Austin partner Gabe MacConaill shares her story." The picture at the top of the article was on the couple's wedding day, both husband and wife beaming, as the sun sets behind them. According to the letter, it was only a month before their ten-year wedding anniversary when Gabe stood in the parking lot of Sidley Austin's Los Angeles office and shot himself in the head, ending his own life. He was forty-two years old.[42]

I slumped back into my seat in disbelief, as I continued reading. The letter goes into detail about all the signs and red flags that foreshadowed Gabe's deteriorating mental health. First, his mentor and confidant announced that he was leaving the firm. Next, one of his partners left to take an early retirement. Both of these incidences caused a cascade of changes within the firm, thrusting Gabe into an important leadership role where he had no lateral support. Finally, Gabe was asked to chair the summer associate program, in which he was

---

41   Ibid.

42   Joanna Litt, "'Big Law Killed My Husband': An Open Letter from a Sidley Partner's Widow," *Law.com: The American Lawyer*, November 12, 2018.

responsible for mentoring thirteen candidates throughout the summer. He felt like he was doing the work of three people.[43]

The acrid taste of guilt washed across my palate. Here I was, throwing a tantrum, having out-of-body experiences, and thinking that my life was about to end over some spilled coffee when there were people out there whose workloads dwarfed my problems. No, they didn't even dwarf my problems. They made them seem microscopic—like particles by comparison. I could not fathom the amount of pressure Gabe MacConaill had experienced before he passed.

As I scanned through the rest of the article, one sentence jumped out at me. It read: "[...] I know 'Big Law' didn't directly kill my husband—because he had a deep, hereditary mental health disorder and lacked essential coping mechanisms. But these influences, coupled with a high-pressure job and a culture where it's shameful to ask for help, shameful to be vulnerable, and shameful not to be perfect, created a perfect storm." This was the key problem. It wasn't just that Gabe had a mental health disorder. He was also in an extremely unsupportive environment that stigmatized mental health so much so that it made him shameful of his condition.

I knew then what I would pitch at the hackathon: a mental health app specifically for law firms that took a top-down management level approach to bettering attorneys' mental health. I glanced at my watch; the two hands formed an acute angle. It was 9:55. No time to come up with questions, so I

---

43   Ibid.

just had to wing it. I quickly dialed Professor Rich's number, and she picked up on the first ring.

Professor Rich was a PhD candidate at USC Marshall School of Business. Her PhD is in strategy, but prior to that she practiced litigation for four years and then compliance work at ICANN (Internet Corporation for Assigned Names and Numbers), a company that does work related to the domain name system. She explained that ICANN was really interesting, but she realized quickly that practicing law wasn't her calling: "I learned a lot about the organization and some of the crazy technical stuff that happens on the back end to see how the internet works, basically. And, I realized, I didn't really care about being a practicing lawyer, and I cared more about technology and innovation. I was just more interested in the business side of everything."

There was a pause. She went on to explain how during her time practicing litigation, she realized her professional life was affecting her relationships in a negative way: "When I did litigation, I did jury trials for an insurance company, which was a fantastic experience, and I enjoyed it a lot. But I realized during this time that I was having more frequent arguments with people who were close to me." It was during one of these arguments with her boyfriend at the time when Professor Rich realized she was becoming an argumentative person and that she was seeing all her interactions as confrontational. "I'm just not very good at separating work and personal life," she added. That's when she decided to transition from litigation to compliance work at ICANN.

I jotted some notes down on a piece of scrap paper. "Okay, gotcha. So, can you explain now the shift from ICANN to your current PhD in strategy? How did that come about?" I asked. "Yeah, so I think at some point I just realized that I was more interested in the business side of everything. Like, even looking back at my litigation experience, I was always trying to extract from the law to come up with a business strategy," she replied. The problem was, Professor Rich didn't really have the quantitative background that most PhD candidates in her field had. She explained that as a lawyer, she had very little exposure to anything that required numbers. But she still applied and got into the program.

Throughout my conversation with Professor Rich, one central theme became clear: that being innovative and thinking creatively can take you far. She explained how there's a lot of lip service given to the flexibility that the juris doctor (JD) degree affords, and that while it may seem like that flexibility only manifests itself later down the line, there's an increasing number of jobs that sit at the intersection of strategy, technology, and law.

For instance, the big three management consultancies (McKinsey & Company, Boston Consulting Group, and Bain & Company) are starting to recruit from law school more. This increase in recruitment of JD candidates has also been propelled by the fact that hiring people right out of law school is cheaper and, since these candidates haven't had law firm experience yet, are generally more malleable in terms of conforming to the consulting firm's culture and expectations.

In addition, innovation has impacted the legal field at a statewide level. Professor Rich explained how certain states are testing out "regulatory sandboxes" in which they're trying out regulations that allow for profit sharing between lawyers and non-lawyers to see how that would impact the structure of law firms and businesses, as well as the economy in general. Utah is one such state that has begun testing out this regulatory sandbox, and California is considering a similar type of regulatory sandbox as well.[44] She went on to recommend a book on the subject: "If you're curious about the topic, I highly suggest you read Gillian Hadfield's book *Rules for a Flat World*. She's a brilliant expert on the topic of the intersection of legal technology and business, so she gets credit for whatever I'm saying about the topic."

Glancing at my watch, I realized I needed to start heading out so I wouldn't be late. I quickly blurted out a final thought: "Absolutely, I will check that out for sure. Last question: What advice do you have for a despondent law student who came out of their 1L year with grades that weren't what they expected?" Without hesitating, she replied "This is so cliché, but your career is long, so be patient and just know that people respect a JD."

She went on to explain the importance of having a foundation of confidence, telling me that in spite of my grade point average, I still had an important perspective to offer. She said, "What I learned in my PhD is being a lawyer gives you a unique perspective on everything, and I think in law school that gets lost because you're only around lawyers. So, you kind of forget that other people don't see the world that way."

---

44   Dan Packel, "Utah Justices Give OK to 'Regulatory Sandbox,'" *Law.com: The American Lawyer*, August 14, 2020.

She further elaborated on the fact that perfectionism in the legal community is a really big problem. Law students are taught to be incredibly meticulous and that they shouldn't voice their opinions unless they're one hundred percent certain that they're right. But in real life, that isn't always the case.

She added: "You should voice your opinion and speak up—you might think you don't have anything to contribute or you're scared, but in business and in life in general, even if you're not one-hundred percent right, people want to hear what you have to say. Your opinion based on your legal training is valuable."

Professor Rich concluded with one final bit of advice: to learn as much as possible about technology and not be afraid to put yourself up for positions that you think you aren't qualified for. Because in all likelihood, you probably can do them. She said, "Perfectionism is a really big problem in the legal field. I didn't think I had the background necessary to do the PhD and even now that I'm in it, I've had to unlearn a lot of that law school perfectionism and lack of confidence. As a lawyer, my inclination was to not speak up unless I was absolutely certain that what I was saying was correct and having to unlearn that has been the most difficult part of the PhD program."

After thanking Professor Rich for her time, I took a moment to digest all her advice. There were so many things I could do with my law degree that I hadn't even thought of until our conversation. I could do consulting, compliance, or even start my own business. But I think the most important lesson was that perfectionism could hinder progress.[45] Professor Rich was someone who had absolutely no knowledge of quantitative sciences, yet she still put herself out there and got into a quant-heavy PhD program. She wasn't the perfect candidate, and she applied anyway and succeeded because she had the confidence to do so. This was some really profound insight.

I then thought to myself, how could this all tie into my mental health app pitch for the hackathon? One topic that both Professor Rich and the Gabe MacConnaill article touched upon was how tough the law firm environment can be. For Professor Rich, it got so bad that friends noticed changes in her behavior. For Gabe, the pressure from work threw him into a deep depression. In both cases, their perfectionism and needing everything to be executed in a precise way led to serious interpersonal and emotional problems.

I tried to reboot my laptop again, aggressively jamming my finger into the power button while blowing on the keyboard with as much lung capacity as I could muster. If my laptop were a patient, it'd probably sue me for medical negligence and intentional inflection of emotional distress. But I was in a hurry and didn't have time to consider my computer's feelings. The machine hummed for a few moments before lighting up and displaying the white apple with a bite taken out of it, the ultimate harbinger of life for any Macbook user. I breathed a sigh of relief. I knew I was supposed to wait for the computer to completely dry before turning on the battery,

---

45   Alice Boyes, "Don't Let Perfection Be the Enemy of Productivity," *Harvard Business Review*, March 3, 2020.

but I was in a rush and needed to be at the Documate office by noon. I quickly logged in and typed down some thoughts, before calling an Uber to Culver City.

The sun was out, but it was still a cool sixty degrees in Culver City. I stared at the tall palm trees from my window—their long finger-like fronds shivering in the breeze. The Uber driver dropped me off at the curb outside the tall glass building. After thanking the driver and exiting the vehicle, I walked through the glass doors and made my way up to the tenth floor. Once I entered the Documate office, it was a completely different scene from when I left it the evening before. There were dozens of new participants and chatting and typing away on their laptops. I spotted a familiar face out of the corner of my eye. It was Michael, a classmate of mine who had told me he was interested in working on MentalBrief with me.

"Hey Michael, what's up?" I asked cheerfully. He yawned and said the same back. "Yeah, I was up late last night brainstorming ideas for our pitch. I've also been talking to a couple people here who were interested in joining our team." He introduced me to two people who were chatting on the couch next to him, "This is Kevin and Catherine." They turned to me to say hello.

Kevin was a senior data scientist at Capgemini, a French multinational consulting firm. He was an experienced coder and would ultimately help us put together the prototype for the web-based version of MentalBrief. Catherine worked as part of the administrative staff at USC and had experience structuring and coding survey questions and distributing them to the student body.

After exchanging contact information and setting up a work-space on Slack, the four of us took over one of Documate's empty breakout rooms and got to work. I explained to them my idea of a mental health app that specifically targeted law firms. I told them that I had thought of the idea after reading the open letter by Gabe MacConaill's widow and how there is such a dearth of mental health resources for attorneys. Everyone in the room nodded in agreement. "I think this is really pertinent now especially, given that there has been such a decline in mental health of lawyers in recent years, and firms just don't care about their attorneys as long as they get their work done," Michael echoed.

We brainstormed for a couple hours before coming up with a three-pronged strategy for our pitch. The MentalBrief app would have three primary functions: a ranking system, an anonymous therapy session counter, and a bonus points calculator.

RANKING SYSTEM

The idea of providing a ranking system for law firms came from Michael, who drew a connection with how law school rankings heavily influence the administration's decisions. "The way the law school structures its grading system, its career services, and on-campus recruitment process all boil down to one thing: U.S. News," he explained. Basically, schools will do whatever they can to get ahead and increase their name recognition. Having a high ranking on the U.S. News & World Report gives prospective law students an incentive to apply to those schools because it promises, at least on the surface level, an opportunity to get ahead professionally and land a lucrative job post-graduation.[46] Applying this logic, a similar type of ranking system for law firms' mental health would encourage firms to take better care of their employees. How would these rankings be organized? Based on the data from Mental-Brief's surveys, our idea was the app would execute, at a firm-wide level, anonymous surveys to the lawyers and staff, asking questions about the firm's culture and mental health initiatives. The survey would consist of multiple choice and short answer questions and, using machine learning and sentiment analysis, the app would generate a "mental health score" to determine how happy the employees were overall. Those scores would then be compared across firms, and the rankings would result from how each firm performed.

"But how are we going to get the attorneys themselves to be proactive in seeking help when they need it?" Catherine interjected. She proceeded to provide some further insight from her experience working with USC administration: "Yeah, a lot of the students at USC, whether law students or graduate students in general, seem to just not want to go to student health to speak to therapists because it's way too time consuming and there's no external incentive other than to better their own mental health. You don't get bonus points in class for taking time out of your day to go to a therapy session, when you could be studying." She reasoned that the same reasoning applies to lawyers and working professionals as well.

---

46   Robert Morse, Ari Castonguay, and Juan Vega-Rodriguez, "Methodology: 2021 Best Law Schools Rankings Find Out How U.S. News Ranks Law Schools," U.S. News & World Report, March 16, 2020.

People already don't have the time or energy to attend therapy sessions, and, if they're not encouraged by the companies they work for to do it, they'll put it off or avoid it altogether. I knew she was right. I had a friend back at Emory tell me stories about how his professor got frustrated with him when he told him that he had to miss a class due to a therapy appointment. We had to think of a solution to stop similar situations from happening at the workplace.

I thought about what mechanisms in school had incentivized me to attend classes and prioritize academics. In most classes throughout my time at Emory, and even in law school, participation counted as part of the overall grade, and students got points for attending and participating in class.

Even though the percentage of participation points toward the overall cumulative grade at the end of the semester was only 5 or 10 percent, it was still enough to motivate me to go. Internally, I thought to myself that each time I attended class, I accrued free points just by showing up, and I gained valuable knowledge that would help me perform better on the final. Participation points were basically small wins designed to incentivize me to get out of bed and go to class.

ANONYMOUS THERAPY SESSION COUNTER

I posed the idea, "What if we gave firms points each time an attorney attends a therapy session? That way, firms will encourage attorneys to attend and the attorneys will be incentivized to attend the sessions because it would help them professionally." Everyone paused for a moment to think about it. "That's a good idea. And we can maybe even add onto that by awarding additional points if attorneys attend consecutive sessions, so that they're incentivized to make therapy a habitual pattern," Michael added. Everyone murmured in agreement, except Catherine. She had her brows furrowed and seemed to be deep in thought.

After a few moments, she said aloud, "I like the idea. But the problem is, even if the attorneys are incentivized and even if the firms are encouraging them to go to therapy sessions, this doesn't really mitigate the amount of pressure and work the attorneys have to get done. I mean, by turning therapy into a professional booster so to speak, aren't we just adding more to their plates?" Catherine had a good point. While therapy is an incredibly useful tool, it can be to the patient's detriment if it's treated as an additional obligation. We needed to come up with a way to make the law firms not only encourage attorneys to get the help they needed but do so in a way that didn't increase their responsibilities and exacerbate their stress.

I reflected on the times in my life when I missed class, despite knowing that it would have an impact on my grade. Was it because I didn't care about losing the points? No. Most of the time I missed classes was a deliberate choice on my part to use that time to catch up on other schoolwork. I remember one very stressful week at Emory, I missed an entire week of classes because I had to finish my honors thesis, and I was overwhelmed with other assignments I had to get done. That was a pretty dark time.

I always wondered why professors didn't speak to one another and coordinate their assignment due dates so they didn't fall on the same day and overwhelm their students. It always frustrated me that there were no mechanisms in place to deter these types of situations from happening, and they seemed to occur repeatedly. Of course, some might argue that it's a teaching lesson, and it's up to the students to organize and use their time wisely. But having a barrage of assignments, exams, and essays with overlapping deadlines thrown at you constantly becomes less of a learning experience and more of a death sentence. And knowing that the stress and pressure only gets worse as a working professional was deeply unsettling. We had to do something to change this.

"What if we penalized law firms?" I blurted out. They looked at me inquisitively. I continued, "I was just thinking there could be a mechanism in place where we deduct points from firms if attorneys have to miss too many therapy sessions specifically due to work-related obligations. This way, we're not punishing the attorneys for having to miss the sessions; instead, the onus falls on the firm to make sure that they're not overworking their employees, or else risk having a lower mental health score and ranking." We all looked at each other and nodded. We were all on board. Perfect.

BONUS POINTS & WELLNESS PLANS

"Okay, one last thing before we start building this thing: I was thinking we could take this all a step further and incentivize firms to provide comprehensive health benefits," Catherine pointed out. She explained her view that taking a more holistic approach to improving mental health would be more effective, given that stress and anxiety are often built up over time from day-to-day interactions. So, firms that offer small things that help make employees' daily lives easier should be rewarded.

Benefits like corporate fitness programs or simply having on-site daycare for working parents, while not directly tied to mental health, can have a tangible effect in improving and mitigating the amount of stress attorneys have to take on. "Sold," Kevin said aloud. We all laughed in agreement. This was perfect. We had our three primary functions and were ready to hack away.

For the rest of the day, we divided into three groups. Kevin worked on creating a web-based platform for the Mental-Brief survey to be executed on, Michael and Catherine brainstormed survey questions, and I worked on the pitch deck and background information on mental health in the legal field. We were all in a state of flow, coordinating seamlessly with one another until the sun set outside.

We heard a knock on the door. It was Professor Moini. "Hey guys, just so you know, you're welcome to stay as long as you like. I think I'm going to head out soon, but feel free to use the space." I glanced at my watch. It was already 9 p.m. "Wow, we really did a lot today," I said with a sigh.

Our pitch was tomorrow morning, and I needed to get a good night's rest. It was a half-hour Uber ride back to my apartment, so I decided to call it a day as well. "I think I'm going to head out now," I told the rest of the group. After wishing them all a good night, I packed my bag and headed down to the lobby.

As I waited outside for my Uber, I felt jittery and excited. Even though I had been working all day, I was still full of go. If our team won first place, we would be able to move on to the second round and then potentially be flown out to the UK to present to judges in the final round. I closed my eyes and imagined myself landing at Heathrow International Airport. I had never been to Europe, but just the thought of traveling internationally to pitch MentalBrief made me want to scream and shout for joy. The Uber driver must've thought I was crazy because I was beaming when he pulled up. "Jesse?" he asked. "Yes. I am Jesse," I said dramatically, as I imagined myself on stage in the UK about to present my pitch for MentalBrief. "Okay... well, get in," he said, as he arched an eyebrow.

Staring out the window of the Honda Civic, I thought to myself, *"This is it. Tomorrow is my moment."* I closed my eyes and visualized the judges naming MentalBrief first place. The crowd erupting with applause. I imagined stepping off the stage to find one of the judges holding my cellphone, alerting me that I was getting a call from One Medical. The voice over the phone would scream enthusiastically, "Jesse, you got the summer associate position!" I imagined working in San Francisco over the summer and inhaling the refreshing, salt-laced breeze from the Bay as I jog down Embarcadero.

I imagined myself purchasing an office space across the street from Google and establishing MentalBrief among the other rising start-ups. I imagined myself typing away in my office, then looking out the window and waving to Marty who'd be eating lunch on the balcony of the building across the street from me. He would wave back and say, "Okay, you're here. Can you get out now?" The Uber driver looked back at me with a look of confusion and annoyance. My wide smile contracted immediately, as I pulled off my headphones. I quickly apologized and clumsily reached for the lever to open the car door.

After he drove off, I began beaming again, as I stood on the sidewalk outside my apartment. "Tomorrow!" I shouted at the top of my lungs. Behind me, a USC security guard looked up from his phone, shaking his head at me in annoyance as I made my way into the building.

CHAPTER 10

THE PITCH

I leapt out of bed and dashed to the closet to put on my suit. Today was the day! Today, I was going to make the best pitch of my life, propelling me to the top of the legal tech start-up ladder. I stole a cursory glance in the mirror and, satisfied with what I saw staring back at me, hurried down the stairs to a red Toyota Corolla waiting for me by the curb. Sitting in the Uber on my way to Culver City, I played "Before I Let Go" from Beyoncé's *Homecoming* live album.

The brass instrumental vibrated through my headphones. I closed my eyes, and I was back on stage. The audience wanted an encore. They wanted me to present the whole thing again, even though they had just heard it. Streamers flew down from the ceiling as Beyoncé crooned through the bridge. The recruiter from One Medical ran into the auditorium flailing her arms and screaming, "Jesse! You did it! We want to offer you the position of CEO at One Medical!"

"Thank you so much!" I said as the entire stage lurched forward.

The audience gasped. I jolted awake.

"You're welcome," my driver replied flatly.

I quickly got out of the car and made my way toward the glass Documate building. The lobby was empty. Either no one had arrived yet, or everyone had already gone upstairs. I walked briskly into the elevator and, when I got to the tenth floor, saw an entirely different scene compared to the evening before. Through the glass walls of the offices, I saw students and developers furiously typing away while chomping down on bagels or guzzling coffee. In the room farthest down the hall, I saw my group already grinding away.

I joined them and got to work immediately. It was crunch time—only a couple hours until the competition, and we had to rehearse our script. I would introduce the team and provide the background on why there is a legal need for a mental health app for law firms. Kevin would then discuss the technical aspects of the prototype he created to execute the survey, Catherine and Michael would talk about the survey questions and points system, and finally I would conclude with future endeavors and Q&A.

After running through the entire presentation three times, we then brainstormed questions the judges might ask us. "The key is to answer as many questions as effectively and concisely as possible," I reminded everyone. This was a tip I had learned from a business communications class I took at Emory. We thought about every angle the judges might quiz us on in terms of our secondary research, the app's programming logic, and even the minutiae of the next steps we were considering for a law school version of MentalBrief in the event that the version for law firms took off. After running through the questions for about an hour, we all felt fairly confident in the delivery and relaxed. As we waited, I casually surfed the web for articles or headlines about mental health in the legal field. We agreed not to bring up Gabe MacConaill, since his death was so recent, and Professor Moini had known him personally. While she wasn't one of the judges, she would still be in the room and bringing up the topic seemed inappropriate.

I scoured JSTOR, HeinOnline, and Google Scholar for law review notes and articles about mental health and suicide among lawyers. There was a wealth of obituaries. One story in particular stuck out to me because it was about an associate at one of the biggest law firms in the US, Skadden, Arps, Slate, Meagher & Flom LLP. Her name was Lisa Johnstone. Lisa was thirty-two years old when she died of an apparent heart attack while she was working remotely at home. In the weeks leading up to her death, her coworkers noted that she had been working overtime and had cut her vacation short to dedicate more time to a case she was working on.[47]

"This story is the perfect opener to our presentation!" I said gleefully as I read the article aloud. Michael looked up from his laptop and then looked away. "What's wrong?" I asked. He paused. "I just feel like we need to treat this project a bit more solemnly. Because it's such a serious topic," he said

---

47   Debra Cassens Weiss, "Did Overwork Kill Skadden Associate? Inconclusive Autopsy Points to Cardiac Issues," *ABA Journal*, November 16, 2011.

sternly. Catherine and Kevin quickly averted their gaze and went back to typing. "Oh…okay," I replied quietly. Not knowing what to say, I became flush with embarrassment. I sheepishly took my iPhone and left the room.

Wandering down the hallway, I attempted to navigate my emotions. "What was that supposed to mean?" I muttered under my breath. "This is supposed to be exciting. This is an exciting project. Like, this app could possibly make history!" I pulled the phone out of my pocket and continued to read the article. One of Lisa's coworkers noted, "We treat ourselves like horses sometimes. I know I did. [...] When my colleague collapsed, I didn't think, 'Wow, there are limits.' I thought: 'Oh nononononono, we're a man down. I'm going to have to work even harder now.'"[48] I stopped pacing. How numb does a person have to become to still be concerned about work when their coworker just passed out in front of them? The author likened the pressure associates face to a thermostat, and how no one knows how much stress they can take before they blow. There's no scale. No gauge. You just keep working until you physically can't anymore. I felt sick to my stomach. I closed my eyes and thought about my family. How would my mom feel?

My mom and dad had sacrificed so much for me to have a better life in America than I would have had I been born in China. If I had a heart attack or some other stress-induced fatal cardiac event from work, how would they feel? They'd be inconsolable. My sister would be inconsolable. I couldn't do that to them. I refused to.

---

48   Ibid.

I scrolled back to the top of the article and read it again. "Lisa…Lisa Johnstone…," I said under my breath. My sister's name is Lisa. I pictured her collapsing at her desk, while her coworkers continued to type away on their laptops. I imagined someone complaining how much more work they would have to do now that she was incapacitated. My eyes grew hot with rage. Then damp with anguish.

I wiped away the droplets and headed back to the breakout room. Michael was right—this was a serious topic that needed to be treated with the sense of solemnity it deserves. Everyone was taking one last look over the slides. After adding some finishing touches to the pitch deck, we heard a knock on the door. It was Professor Moini. "You guys are up! Best of luck," she said cheerfully. My palms suddenly got sweaty. This was it. We walked out of the breakout room and down the hallway. The three judges smiled at us as we entered the room.

The center of the room had a long table. The judges and other teams sat on one side of it, while the TV monitor hung on the wall on the opposite side. It was a flat screen TV, with an HDMI cord for us to connect to our laptops. I nervously stuck the cord into the socket of my Macbook and opened the slide deck, as the monitor flashed on. "We're ready whenever you are," one of the judges said, her voice echoing from the far side of the room. I took a deep breath, counted to three, and began. "Thank you all so much for being here today…." We went through the slides and transitioned among each other exactly as planned. Our points were crystal clear. As we got to the last slide, the giddiness I felt from earlier that morning returned. "Now, we'd like to open the floor up for questions.

Thank you!" I said with a smile. The judges applauded and began flipping through their notes.

While the other judges scribbled on their notepads, the judge on the far left began without hesitation. "So, how exactly do you plan on getting the law firms on board with this app? I mean, I worked as a litigator for over a decade and the amount of work isn't going to just disappear. There's just a lot that needs to be done, and if people have to work overtime, then that's the way it is." We all looked at each other, wide-eyed. I cleared my throat. "Well, that's an excellent point but given that young attorneys and law students are increasingly valuing and prioritizing finding work at firms that care about their mental health and work life balance, MentalBrief is a great way for firms to attract those prospective candidates." Catherine, Michael, and Kevin nodded in agreement.

The judge was unfazed, "The thing is, stress is a natural part of any big law firm. Work-life balance isn't a priority in these types of environments, so I'm guessing based on the algorithm your product is using, all of the firms' mental health scores are going to be pretty abysmal. And if that's the case, there's just no way that a partner would want to implement the app, let alone make the score reports public."

Catherine chimed in, "Even though the attorneys may set relatively low scores based on their responses to the surveys, the firm's overall score may actually be higher and, perhaps, more palatable to the public, given the bonus points mechanisms we have in place. For instance, if a firm has a corporate wellness plan or an in-house counselor, these points can accrue and give the firm a big boost."

The judge nodded, "Okay. I see your point."

The rest of the Q&A session was a blur. The other two judges asked relatively soft-ball questions about our future endeavors and how we planned on partnering with U.S. News or Vault to publicize and gamify the participating firms' mental health ranking. Overall, though, we felt good. It was a job well done.

After leaving the room, we chatted with a few of the other participants and relaxed. I felt confident. I still thought we had a pretty good chance of getting first place. After about a half hour, the judges walked out of the room, one of them with a slip of paper in her hand. Professor Moini called everyone's attention. "Thank you all for participating in the 2020 Global Legal Hackathon. We thought all of your projects were phenomenal, and we were really impressed with all of the effort you all put in. So great job!"

The judge holding the slip of paper began reading the top three results. I closed my eyes. Beyoncé started singing in my head. Confetti showered from the ceiling. The brass fanfare echoed and cascaded throughout the halls. Her marching band came out, as she began singing the final verse of "Before I Let Go."

"Third place and second-runner up is...."

It would suck to be third place, I thought to myself. Could never be us.

"MentalBrief," she announced.

"Nice try, MentalBrief," I chuckled to myself.

"Better luck next ti—"

The band abruptly stopped.

Beyoncé shook her head as she walked off stage. The auditorium went dark. I looked over at my teammates in horror and they looked back, our mouths agape. Michael reflexively began clapping, mustering a weak, but cheerful, affirmation of our hard work. "Good job, team, good job. Third place. Not bad at all." I closed my mouth and stared blankly at the wall.

"Third place. We got third," I repeated to myself over and over again. This must've been how Haley Reinhart felt when she ended up third place on American Idol… or Elizabeth Warren when she dropped out of the 2020 presidential race after placing behind Biden and Bernie. I shook my head in disbelief, ignoring everyone around me trying to console me. The judge's voice blurred into the background. We weren't moving onto the next round. We weren't going to the UK. The private jet to Heathrow wasn't coming. I quietly thanked the team, threw all my belongings haphazardly into my backpack, and ran downstairs to catch an Uber. As I sprinted down the steps, my eyes felt hot again. I furrowed my eyebrows, trying to push the droplets back down my tear ducts. I was angry. I was furious. I was sad. I was lost.

I stared out the window of my Uber. The tall glass building shrank in the distance as we drove off. I put on my headphones as "You Can't Always Get What You Want" by the Rolling Stones began playing. The opening voices of The London Bach Choir singing the song title reminded me of the perennial sound bite I'd heard continually since the first day I set foot in the law school—Jesse, you can't get what you want.

Streetlamps flew past my view; each greeting me for a split second before disappearing into the distance. As the song reached the bridge and Brian Jones' fingers tinkered mockingly on the higher end of the keyboard, I started sobbing again. This time, inconsolably. I thought about everything that had led up to this moment and tried to parse out the positives.

I had founded a new student organization, enrolled in a great class, and met some interesting people. But every time a glimmer of hope sparked from one of those positive thoughts, it seemed like an onslaught of misery would descend from above and extinguish it. My summer job situation was still up in the air, my GPA was trash, I hadn't determined what type of law I wanted to practice, and now I had just lost the hackathon that I was banking on to change my life. Somehow cutting through all this despair, one emotion stuck out like an infected limb—I was profoundly lonely.

Everyone else was lightyears ahead of me, and no matter how hard I tried to scrub and cleanse myself of the pre-determined fate that the career counselors and professors had tattooed on my forehead, the ink just wouldn't come off. It couldn't. It was permanent. It was a scarlet "A" for Average. Or, perhaps, "A" for Amateur. "A" for ashtray…aimless… absent-minded…a-dumbass…a-dilettante…a person who couldn't come up with more than five adjectives starting with the letter A. A defect. That's what my tombstone should read. There was no softening the blow—I felt like shit. And in that moment, I was shit. Everything I did was shit and everything was hopeless.

I didn't get out of bed the next day, except when my Grubhub order arrived, or when I needed to relieve myself. I binged a couple shows on Netflix and stuffed my face with those mint ice-cream bites from Trader Joe's. As I got to the season finale of *On My Block*, I felt my phone vibrate. It was an email from One Medical.

I jolted upright and opened the notification. "Thank you for applying for the Legal Summer Associate role. We are honored that you want to contribute to our mission to transform health care." This didn't sound promising. I took one long swipe with my thumb and read the text at the bottom: "At this time, we have decided to move forward with other candidates whose experience more closely aligns with the skill sets we are looking for." I threw my phone across the room, curled up into a fetal position, and wept. "They always say, misfortune comes in threes!" I yelled at the ceiling. "You really got me this time, universe!"

My roommate walked in, watched me sobbing inconsolably for a few moments, rolled his eyes, and walked out, closing the door behind him. After spending the entire day in a depressive trance, I pinched up what little remained of my strength and dignity, like two grains of rice, and forced myself to go to class. I couldn't mope around forever but getting back into the swing of things was harder than expected.

The week after the hackathon was likely the most difficult one of my law school career. I was very depressed, and my brain was desperate for dopamine. It didn't matter how much, I just needed something—anything to feel like I was still remotely competent. I frantically applied for jobs in between classes, editing dozens of cover letters and shooting them out at lightning speed. I was in a frenzy, stopping only once in a while to eat or weep in the bathroom. But once I was done feeling sorry for myself, I lugged my depression-infected body back to my seat and kept working. I had to win at least once, like Angela Duckworth said. A small win. A foot in the door. All the while, I also thought intently about what my ultimate concern might be. Clearly it was to be successful, but it had to be more specific than that. What was a goal or project that I so intensely wanted to accomplish that I would go to the ends of the earth to make it happen? Back at the hackathon, I thought it was mental health. MentalBrief gave me a sense of purpose. It gave meaning to everything I did at the time. But now that the hackathon was over and I had lost, what could I do to improve mental health in the legal profession?

Late one evening, after everyone else in the library had left, I was typing away furiously on the third floor trying to finish a few more cover letters when I heard a ping. It was an email from the Student Bar Association. Ignoring it at first, because I knew if I got distracted, I'd never finish on time, I kept typing. A few moments later, my phone, which had been annoyingly set to ring twice if I didn't open a notification the first time, pinged again.

I let out an exasperated sigh, reached into my pocket, and began reading the message. "Hi Members of the Class of

2021 and the Class of 2022, I hope everyone and their families are doing well. SBA Elections are here! SBA is the largest and oldest student organization at Gould." My eyes widened. I sat up straight and thought to myself, "I'm going to run for President."

CHAPTER 11

DON'T SWEAT THE SHINY STUFF

————

My alarm rang. I hit snooze and rolled over, drifting back asleep. It rang again. I groaned and tried to hit snooze again, but accidentally knocked my phone off the nightstand. I peered over the edge of my bed as the screen lit up. The digital clock glowed in my face. It was 9:05. I was late for class.

It was the last week of March, and it had been raining for the past four days in Los Angeles. For some reason I never thought to purchase an umbrella because I thought it wasn't supposed to ever rain. When I reached the entrance of my apartment, I saw that it was pouring outside. Taking a deep breath like I was about to make my debut as an Olympic diver, I bolted out the door and sprinted across the street to school. Since I lived so close to campus, I was only in the rain for a few minutes. But when I made it to the lecture hall, I was drenched. I panted to catch my breath before entering the room, so as not to make a scene. Rainwater coated every inch of my body, clinging to my hair and limbs like a cloak of misfortune. *"At least the weather matches how I feel,"* I thought to myself.

I sat through the lecture, listlessly surfing the internet. Behind me, I heard some classmates whispering something about virtual remote classes starting the following week. "I think Dean Guzman is going to make an announcement later this week," one of them said.

Class ended, and I made my way up the staircase by the front entrance and to the library to catch up on some readings for a few hours before my next class, Legal Innovations Lab, which began at 6 p.m. Legal Innovations was my only evening class, and it typically ended around 9 p.m. That day, Professor Moini had invited a CEO and USC alum, Rick Merrill, to come in and talk to the class about his start-up, 'Gavelytics.'[49] At around 5:45 p.m., I got up and slowly made my way to the classroom for the lecture, dragging my feet the entire time. The rainwater had dried on me, and I smelled like wet dog. I was still feeling despondent about the one-two-punch of the hackathon and One Medical debacles, and, while I had at least some newfound inspiration in knowing that I would be running for SBA president, my mood was still a net negative after aggregating the sum of my emotions.

As I entered the room, I saw Rick standing at the front of the class, setting up his PowerPoint presentation on the computer. He was tall and wore a navy blue suit. Everything about his appearance looked really professional—his hair was perfectly

---

49   Kevin O'Keefe, "Rick Merrill, CEO of Gavelytics, on Executing an Idea," *Legal Tech Founders*, September 17, 2018.

combed, his brown leather shoes shined. He reminded me a bit of Harvey Spector, a character from the TV show *Suits*. I assumed he was going to give a lecture about the importance of honing our legal research skills and having a well-crafted résumé, so I took out my laptop and got ready to tune him out as he began speaking.

"What if I told you that even if you had the perfect legal argument, cited the best case law, and delivered in the most convincing manner, that the judge still might not rule in your favor." I paused right before typing in my password. He went on to tell a story about two bench trials—that is, a trial by judge, as opposed to a trial in front of a jury—that he had. In both of those trials, Rick was confident that he had the better facts, the better legal team, and the better strategy. Everything seemed to point to an easy victory. But when the judges gave their decisions, Rick lost. Badly.

He elaborated, "We honestly felt—and I still feel to this day— that we were the better team, and we should have won. But the judge just didn't like us or didn't agree with our argument." "Isn't it the judge's duty to make their decisions objectively?" one student interjected. "Trial judges have a lot of discretion," Rick replied, "and the reality is, the only check on that discretion is the court of appeals. So, the trial judges, basically, can do what they want. That's why we founded Gavelytics."

Gavelytics is a data analysis tool that helps predict judges' decisions.[50] Rick likened Gavelytics to sports statistics: "So what Gavelytics does is it understands how the judge

---

50   "About Us," Gavelytics, accessed September 12, 2020.

applies the law. Like in baseball, you can measure all kinds of things—you can measure how well a certain batter hits left-handed pitching versus how well they hit right-handed pitching. It occurred to me that these types of statistics can help predict judges' decisions as well. And the statistics we found are astounding." He went on to explain how some judges may be more likely to grant a motion for summary judgement for certain business tort cases if a particular case law is cited. Other judges may tend to simply favor plaintiffs over defendants, regardless of how good the defendant's legal arguments may be. And so on and so forth.

As I processed everything Rick was teaching us, I felt a range of emotions. On the one hand, I was relieved to hear him tell us that even the best, highest-paid, most diligent lawyer in the room could lose at the trial level. Since I knew I would never be at the top of my class or make it to the upper echelon of big law firms, it was comforting to know that even if I did, that still didn't guarantee success in a court of law. On the other hand, I was frustrated and angry because what Rick was saying basically was that the legal system wasn't a completely fool-proof, merit-based system. The best legal team didn't always win, and judges could make bad calls.

So, did that mean there really wasn't any real incentive to work incredibly hard to make it to the top, because you wouldn't necessarily be rewarded for it? If so, what was the point of all of this? What was the purpose behind grinding through three grueling years of law school, going through OCI, and finally getting hired by a big law firm? For what? To be angry and miserable and put up with petty bullshit every single day until you retire? Is that all we have to live for? Maybe I was missing a bigger point.

I raised my hand and asked, "So…what is the end game then?" He looked back, seemingly confused by the question, so I kept going. "I mean, taking money out of the equation, why is it so important to work so hard to get a great GPA and land an offer at a big law firm if the judge is just going to say 'no' because he's having a bad day? If being the most perfect, brilliant legal genius in the room isn't going to guarantee a win, then doesn't that disincentivize striving to get straight A's in law school?"

He paused for a moment to think. "Perhaps, don't place so much weight on grades in general. I mean, that's easier said than done—when I was in law school, I was stressed out because of my grades, which were not the greatest. But I think the true value of law school is learning how to think analytically and logically. That's the sort of 'mental software' so to speak that is valuable way beyond what a transcript or brand name law firm says about you. It's about thinking as a lawyer. Applying all of the facts." I nodded in agreement.

That was a good point—placing too much emphasis on prestige and status can be a really toxic approach to life. I guess that was the message all along—to focus simply on being a good lawyer all around. Rick continued, "It's also about the people you meet. Go meet as many people as you can. Be a nice guy! These are your future colleagues—they'll send you business, so just get to know your professors, your classmates in the class above you, below you, wherever. All those things. That's a ton of value of law school because before you know it, your buddies will be working at some firm and they can hire you or send you a case or whatever. They might call you up and say, 'Hey, I'm working on a case. Come work for me,' and that is something so valuable. I think if you focus on those things, life will work out okay."

He didn't say it exactly, but the phrase that kept popping up in my head was "don't sweat the shiny stuff." The money, the perfect transcript, the title of the law firm. Those things come and go. What remained constant and what guaranteed your eventual success were your friendships, your network, and your personality. Law school was a gigantic networking opportunity. Getting an A, B, or even a C in a class or two couldn't diminish the value in being a law student at a top-twenty law school. When class ended, I left the room feeling exhausted. The pain of my failures from earlier still stung, but it was much duller and less jarring than it was before. As I walked across the street away from the law school, I found myself repeating the phrase under my breath: "Don't sweat the shiny stuff…Don't sweat the shiny stuff."

I stood in the lobby waiting for the elevator car to come down the shaft. I pulled out my phone and listlessly scrolled through my Twitter feed when a notification banner appeared at the top of my screen. It was an email from the dean of the law school. Skimming through the message, my eyes widened. "As the Provost's memo indicates, the university—including Gould School of Law—will hold classes online starting tomorrow. Students are encouraged not to return to campus and, instead, take their classes remotely until further notice." Remote classes? I had never done anything longer than an interview remotely. How could the professors possibly teach us for two hours straight through Skype? Also, how were we going to have the Student Bar Association election? Would we even have it at all? Just when I thought I was making some modicum of progress toward feeling better, the universe was stopping me in my tracks yet again.

CHAPTER 12

LADY EBOSHI AND THE FOREST SPIRIT

———

The following weeks after USC switched to remote teaching seemed to emulate a domino effect. Everything began shutting down one by one. The gyms, the stores, the restaurants. Students who had left the country for spring break weren't allowed back on campus even to retrieve their belongings. My roommates and I became confined within our apartment. We passed the time by cooking meals and doing home workouts together. When I was feeling especially overwhelmed, I would often FaceTime or set up Zoom dates with friends.

The pandemic reminded me of a scene from the film *Princess Mononoke* by Hayao Miyazaki.[51] In one of the final clips, the leader of the villagers Lady Eboshi, who represents mankind's industrialization and modernity, finally kills the Great Forest Spirit, which was basically this deer-like creature with a human face. When Eboshi beheads the spirit by shooting a

———

51 *Princess Mononoke*, IMDb, accessed September 12, 2020.

bullet straight through its skull, a wave of toxic sludge pours out of its body and washes over the entirety of Eboshi's village and surrounding forest, destroying everything in its path.

The distinct imagery and stark contrast between Eboshi and the Spirit reminded me of the tension between law school and the world at large. Eboshi wasn't an inherently evil character—she wanted to kill the Spirit because she believed its blood would cure the sick people living in her village. To me, she represented productivity, technology, machinery, and man's eternal fight to create a fertile and prolific society. The Spirit represented nature, and, at least from my interpretation, its death and resulting destruction symbolized how utterly helpless we as humans are when it comes to the sheer power of nature and biology.[52]

Here I was, caught up mentally and emotionally over my journey in law school and my quandary over whether or not I would find success as a lawyer, and seemingly out of nowhere, a global pandemic caused by a mysterious virus wiped everything out, like the wave of toxic sludge from the movie. It was incredible. It was alarming. And most of all, it was a wake-up call that in the grand scheme of things, there were bigger problems out there. And I couldn't afford to be throwing fits like a toddler over small losses.

How I felt about my circumstances or how setbacks affected me emotionally weren't going to change the reality, which was that life would go on and the world could change in the

---

52 Janet Maslin, "FILM REVIEW; Waging a Mythic Battle to Preserve a Pristine Forest," *New York Times*, September 27, 1999.

blink of an eye. People were losing their jobs, their homes, their ability to feed themselves; some were dying. I could be one of them, and my GPA wasn't going to change whether I would be or not. At the end of the movie, Lady Eboshi doesn't die, although she does get her arm bitten off by an angry wolf spirit, and she lives on to rebuild the village.

One night after a particularly anxiety-provoking day of video conferences and Zoom lectures, I called my friend Gabby to chat and unwind at the end of the day. Gabby and I were in the same small section our first year in law school—section "M." In a way, I feel as though Gabby and I will be interminably linked for the rest of our lives by the highs and lows that made up our 1L experience together. "Do you remember how we first met?" I asked through my laptop's microphone. We both burst out laughing.

We met on the second day of orientation. I had missed the first day because I flew in directly from China, where I was visiting relatives in Hubei. My small section was sitting in a circle outside the law school doing icebreakers, and I walked over to join the conversation. Sometime later, Gabby told me that everyone was confused as to who I was because no one had seen me the first day and my name was missing from the roster. "Allison literally texted the GroupMe for our small section and was like, 'Who is this kid?'" she said, stifling a laugh. Allison was our peer mentor. Usually second year students go through an application process to become mentors for the 1Ls; each small section usually has two mentors.

As we chatted, we reminisced on some of the darker moments of law school. We talked about how, before entering law school, we both thought it would be a complete cake walk, despite everyone warning us not to be too confident. "Everyone warned me—like even my dad kept saying to me, 'Oh, don't expect to be the big fish,' but I just didn't listen!" Much to Gabby's chagrin, by the end of her first semester in law school, she had performed below median in every course, ending up with around a 3.1—roughly the same as my own GPA. She was devastated. "I just remember thinking to myself, wow I really poured myself into that semester. I worked every day. I would wake up, do homework, read, study, go to school, eat, and then study again." I nodded, knowingly. She continued, "I would go to professors and at one point one of them even said I was doing 'excellently,' and that I should consider doing a clerkship."

But Gabby's experience was actually far more traumatic than simply getting a bad grade. For Gabby, grades were a part of her identity. They were a way for her to survive. To escape. To feel worthy. Throughout her childhood, Gabby experienced a series of unfortunate events that significantly shaped her outlook on life. When she was eight, her parents got a divorce—a nasty one that resulted in both parents having to go to family court every year and uprooted her and her younger sister's lives.

She eventually ended up moving to Texas to live with her mother and attended a strict Roman Catholic private school. "It was hard transitioning from a two-parent household to a single-parent household. Like, not only was it a less comfortable situation financially, but living with my mother who didn't go to college presented its own issues." She explained how being thrust into such an academically rigorous private school without anybody at home who could help forced her to become extremely independent in terms of getting schoolwork done. And while her mother and father were constantly feuding and having legal battles, school became Gabby's refuge. "I pretty much poured myself into school, extracurriculars, clubs, anything that I felt like would give me outward validation that I couldn't get from my parents."

So, when Gabby got her first semester grades back in law school, it wasn't just a blow to her ego—it was a blow to her identity. School was the only constant Gabby had ever known, and without it, there was nothing stable for her to grab onto. In fact, seeing how poorly she had performed made Gabby question, just like I did, whether or not she really belonged at law school in the first place, whether she was truly as smart as she had always believed she was, or if she had any control over her life at all. It triggered and uncovered some of her darkest, most suppressed memories from high school and living with her mother. "My mom…she was pretty manipulative. And living with her was always a toxic and stressful experience. The worst was when I got really sick my junior year of high school."

During her junior year, Gabby was diagnosed with mononucleosis and had to stay home for two months, where she was isolated from her friends, had little to no contact with her sister who lived in the same house, and ended up losing twenty pounds due to her condition. It was at the weakest, most feeble point in her life, both emotionally and physically. And to make matters worse, during her two-month isolation, Gabby became severely depressed and even suicidal. "I had literally no one at that point. I was isolated. It was very traumatic, being only sixteen years old. I had little to no contact with my dad, and my sister was in the house but wasn't allowed to talk to me."

Despite these circumstances, however, there was one positive outcome. After recovering enough to attend school, Gabby attended the last three weeks of classes and took her finals. She got straight A's on all of them. "I think that was the moment when I realized how much power I had—like, in terms of the level of control and mastery I possessed when it came to school. Nobody knew I was going through all these traumatic experiences. I was in survival mode the entire time. It was like an adrenaline thing—even though I was so weak and isolated, I knew the only way I could get out of my predicament was to do well in school. And so, I did."

This stubborn work ethic and intense drive to succeed academically followed Gabby the following year, in spite of another major setback that arose. Because Gabby had missed so much school and had not had time to prepare for the ACT, she decided to repeat her junior year. And while that decision was ultimately a salubrious one for her mental and physical health, it gave way to a host of unexpected problems at school. "It was a small, predominantly white Catholic school. I'm half black and half Guyanese— my mom's from Guyana, which is a small country in South America. I'm a bit racially ambiguous, especially because my last name is 'Rodrigues,' so people assume I'm Latina, but it's actually a Portuguese surname. Either way, people knew I wasn't white, and that definitely played a part in a lot of the racially charged rumors and assumptions that were spread about me at school."

When Gabby repeated her junior year, she was absolutely mortified when she heard that people were spreading lies about her, saying she was dumb and that she was repeating the year because she was too stupid. No one had any idea the amount of hardships she was facing at home, not to mention the serious medical condition she had only recently recovered from. Instead, they all assumed she missed school because classes were too hard for her and she didn't have the willingness to continue. To make matters worse, she received mixed reactions to her decision at home. She explained, "My dad was really supportive in my decision. He thought it was best for me to rest up and take another year so that I could get into the best college possible. But my mom wanted me to just apply and finish high school as soon as possible." By the time her senior year came around, Gabby decided to transfer to a public school.

"So, by the time I got to public school my senior year, I had ended up getting a really good ACT score, and I had my sights set on UT Austin, which is a really selective school. But, in spite of my high grades at a prestigious private school and strong ACT score, for some reason my college counselor wasn't that supportive." Gabby's counselor at the public school basically told her that she needed to set her sights lower; that UT Austin was too high a reach for her.

It was yet another frustrating setback for Gabby. Yet another individual in her life who was supposed to support her dreams, who instead didn't believe in her and was telling her that she didn't have the ability to win. Again, however, Gabby refused to take no for an answer. She buried her head in schoolwork and made it her mission to prove to all the people who told her she'd never make it—her private school classmates, her counselor, her own mother—that they were wrong. She ended up getting her acceptance letter in the mail.

"Finally. Like—finally I wasn't an impostor anymore. I wasn't 'the girl who got left behind and had to repeat a year,' I wasn't the 'girl who was being lazy for not rushing to apply for colleges.' That girl wasn't me. No, I was finally 'the girl who got into UT Austin, who grit her teeth and kept pushing despite everyone telling her she was a nobody.'" Academic success gave Gabby confidence in herself. It gave her access—access to the comfort and love she had been deprived of her entire life. It gave her a sense of belonging. She was a scholar, a fighter, a winner. Fast forward to the end of fall 2018—the image of herself that Gabby had painstakingly assembled through her sheer willpower was shattered.

This was a chapter of her story Gabby had never read before. It was completely uncharted territory. The tectonic plates of her family and social life, at home and in school, were always shifting and quaking beneath her. But grades were always bolted down to the Earth's core with titanium clamps and Gorilla Glue. That is, until law school.

"I felt impostor syndrome like I had never felt before in my life. In high school and even throughout college, even though there were some massive obstacles and the outcome looked entirely hopeless, my grades would come back, and everything would be okay. So, this was like experiencing all those traumatic events and hardships, except with the revised outcome of not having good grades to save me from my peril." Gabby likened her first year of law school to a simulation of her entire life in one year. She felt like she had completely blown it. That all her opportunities were now completely out the window.

And it wasn't just the fact that her grades were low; it was also the way she received them that really set her over the edge. "I remember getting an email on New Year's Eve sometime in the evening. I was with my family, and my dad had spent a grand on dinner, and we were all just enjoying the holiday together. And when I opened it up to read it...my heart just sank. It was a really callously worded message from the head of the legal writing department who basically said that based on a preliminary review of the fall semester exams, I was being recommended by my professors to take remedial criminal law to get extra practice in legal writing and analysis for the spring semester." Gabby described the email as a "gut-punch." A feeling that not everyone could understand.

She elaborated, "Going through law school is such a unique experience that no matter how much it's broken down and distilled, those who don't experience it firsthand just will not be able to comprehend the pressure and anxiety that comes with being a 1L." Gabby described that the anxiety and frustration was always at the brink of overflowing. It had gotten so bad that even before she got the email, she had started screaming and had burst into tears because they had run out of rice at the dinner table. "Like, it was plain old, regular white rice. That was what I was freaking out over. I was like, well damn, first I have to go through a semester of hell, and now I can't even get some white rice?" Gabby felt like a complete impostor. And the email felt like a grim reminder of her high school counselor. Except the sound bite now was slightly altered from "you won't be able to get into UT Austin" to "you won't be able to become a great lawyer."

Still, Gabby had always been a fighter. She was the fearless Lady Eboshi, driven to succeed and conquer at all costs. She built an entire village with her bare hands and was ready to sacrifice everything to preserve it. Her survival instincts kicked in. When the second semester of 1L year finally came, Gabby knew the drill. She was Lady Eboshi, clearing a path in front of her so she could get a clear shot at the Forest Spirit's head—the prestige of having a strong GPA coming out of 1L year. "When I went back, I just didn't prioritize my mental health at all. I just thought I could plow through and come out the other side like I did in the past. And that... that just did not work." Gabby worked even harder her second semester. She had one goal in mind and one goal only: to redeem herself. To prove that she belonged. She stopped speaking to her therapist, stopped attending social events, and even distanced herself from those she regularly spoke to the semester before. That semester, Gabby ended up getting even lower grades than she got in the fall. Not only had she sacrificed her overall well-being and a significant amount of time and energy, but for the first time in her life, Gabby had absolutely nothing to show for it.

The toxic sludge poured from the Forest Spirit's head and took the light out of almost every part of Gabby's life. By the end of the spring semester, Gabby was down and out. She was numb. "It was a really sad time for me. I mean, luckily before law school, I got that Sidley/Amazon fellowship, so I had my summer job. But I felt completely incompetent and self-conscious. Like, I felt like I was the token diversity hire who was just there for the photo ops, but not because of any of my merits." To make matters worse, by the time OCI came around, Gabby had to go through the frustrating process of having to explain her transcript to prospective employers. But before that could happen, she got a call. "So, two days before OCI, I miraculously got a return offer from Sidley and had gotten really good reviews for the work that I did because I really did try my best that summer even though I was feeling really down the entire time. But because I got the offer so close to my interviews, I couldn't reschedule them and had to do three of the ones I registered for."

Gabby's second interview was with an international law firm with over 900 attorneys. In the middle of the interview, one of the senior associates stopped his co-interviewer mid-sentence and made a very exaggerated motion with his pen, as he circled something on Gabby's application. He then looked at her and asked, "You clearly appear to be very articulate and professional, but can you explain to me how your grades are the way that they are?" Gabby was taken aback.

It wasn't that she didn't expect the question to be asked; it was the tone and manner the interviewer asked it. "It felt demeaning and kind of aggressive. Like, I know GPA is important, and obviously it was something I was concerned about, but he literally stopped the interview to ask this question—as though continuing any conversation with me at all was pointless until I could clarify why my grades were low. I mean, clearly, I had other things that I could offer. But to think that they would completely reduce me to a number was just an awful feeling."

Once OCI concluded, Gabby was completely drained. The only good news was that she had the offer to return to Sidley. But that offer was contingent upon her getting a certain GPA cutoff—a cutoff that Gabby felt she couldn't get. And as the toxic sludge flowed freely through her village, it flooded her home as well. Gabby's father was diagnosed with cancer, which required footing an enormous medical bill. Now, not only was Gabby anxious about getting her return offer at Sidley, she had the added pressure of her father's health condition, as well as the stress of having to go even further into debt since her father couldn't support her financially anymore.

There she stood, gazing at the horizon. Where once there was a booming society of industrious villagers now lay a desolate wasteland. A gust of wind blew past her, causing her robes to flutter violently as if to catch their breath before growing still. Blood dripped from the open wound where her arm had been bitten off by the wolf spirit. Everything Lady Eboshi had built was gone. But now she had a new opportunity. A chance to create a different society, one that was less obsessed with progress and success. One that focused, instead, on wellness and improvement.

The following fall semester of her 2L year, Gabby took a step back and did the exact opposite of what she had done before. Instead of focusing on school, she began taking care of herself. She took a reduced load of classes to give herself some room to breathe, and she even got an emotional support animal—a puppy affectionately named Thor. In addition, Gabby began reframing her mindset. Through her therapy sessions and journaling, Gabby began delving into and questioning where her anxiety really stemmed from. Why was she so concerned about success and big law? "One thing I realized was that I had really bad tunnel vision. Like, I was really only focused on big law or getting a federal clerkship after law school. But that only happens to maybe like ten students. What happens to the rest of the student body? Not everyone is going to be able to get a 4.0 and clerk or work at Cravath or Sullivan & Cromwell. That's just not possible. But we can all be just as happy and content with whatever position we do end up at. So, I think realizing that I can be just as successful and happy somewhere other than Sidley, so long as I gave my best effort and fought to improve myself, gave me a sense of comfort."

Gabby also took time throughout the fall of her 2L year to reflect upon being in the remedial criminal law class. "I remember looking around the room of that class and seeing how almost everyone was a student of color or person from a marginalized background." Those were the people who struggled the most in high school. Those who grew up in the least ideal circumstances, who faced bullying or discrimination growing up, and who didn't have access to the same resources as their more affluent, privileged classmates. But what made that class so special was that each and every one of those students were all the more likely to succeed and thrive in life. Because it took a special kind of person to land at the bottom of the class, be told that they were dumb and needed extra help and choose to stay in law school. They were demonstrating their grit simply by showing up!

Those were the people, in Gabby's mind, who had the best ability to be successful in the long run. To hustle. To get a job. To be well-rounded. They had to cultivate a myriad of other talents and skills that their classmates who got 4.0s on their transcripts never developed because they couldn't rely on their GPAs to get jobs. "We bring a type of dedication, work ethic, resilience, and so many other assets to the table that those who ended up at the top of the class don't have. That's what makes us different."

When final exams were just around the corner, Gabby for the first time felt a sense of peace. She wasn't overly concerned about how she would perform, and while the pressure to do well was certainly greater than it had ever been before, she felt mentally prepared to take on whatever came her way. Then, the day before finals, Gabby got into a car accident. "Right as finals season started, someone backed into my car as they were pulling out of the garage, which landed me in urgent care for eight hours. Turns out I had a herniated disk and had to wear a neck brace for six weeks." Though she felt hopeless, Gabby was never one to give up completely. "I just had to give myself a break. I physically could only give 60 to 70 percent of myself to school because of my injuries, so even though the inner me who's never settled for less than 100 percent and who wanted to give 110 percent to these exams was shouting in the back of my head to get back up and push, I just had to let that expectation go. And that was the most freeing thing I could do for myself."

Letting go of the need to be perfect allowed Gabby to finally unfetter herself from the fear of inadequacy that had haunted her throughout her life. "I let go of the pressure of trying to get the best grades. At that point, I was just in the mindset of 'I'm gonna get the grades that I get and I'm gonna do the best that I can. And that's all I can ask of myself at this juncture.'" So, Gabby trudged forward through the sludge, accepting whatever her fate decided. She took all her exams on time with the rest of her classmates. And when she got her grades back, she received the best grades she had gotten since coming to law school. "I got a 3.50, and even got a 3.80 in one of my legal writing classes! I think the moral is that even though everything fell apart at the last minute, I was able to get through it because I had spent the entire semester taking care of myself, finding inner peace, speaking with my therapist, and prioritizing my health above all else. That was what got me through and that's what made all the difference when it really became do or die."

She did it. Lady Eboshi made her triumphant comeback, reforming a village that focused less on extrinsic motivators like results and productivity, and more on personal development, growth, and mental wellness. Everything in Gabby's life always felt like an "all or nothing" situation. She was either the best of the best academically or she was worthless and incompetent. By letting go of that dichotomy and focusing on improvement over all else, Gabby was able to finally realize her fullest potential. The point wasn't that she ended up getting the grades she wanted. Rather, Gabby's success was the result of her being able to finally see herself as a person deserving of a full and happy life, regardless of how she performed academically.

After my conversation with Gabby, I knew immediately that this was the mindset that I needed to have. Not just in the context of law school, not just throughout my career, and not just in my personal life, but for life as a whole—for all of the above. I needed to acknowledge that, at my core, no matter how poorly I performed in school, no matter what kind of job I landed (if any), and no matter how few votes I got in the election, that I was a person worthy and deserving of love. I deserved a happy and fulfilling life.

My performance academically and professionally would always be completely separate from that. Heading into election season, I had no idea what my chances of winning were. All I knew was, whether I won or lost, the result would have zero impact on my self-worth. I refused to allow it.

CHAPTER 13

KIRA-KIRA

I remember in the fifth grade I did a book report on a book titled *Kira-Kira* by Cynthia Kadohata.[53] The story is about two Japanese American sisters from Georgia. The older sister, Lynn, is perfect. She gets straight A's and is the star of the family. The younger sister, Katie, is the opposite. She's a C-student, incredibly lazy, and constantly being chastised by her parents and teachers for behaving irresponsibly. Lynn gets diagnosed with lymphoma and passes away. As a result, Katie starts to try harder and eventually becomes the mature, independent, and straight-A daughter her parents always wanted her to be. The title, and Lynn's catchphrase, "Kira-Kira," is actually a Japanese term that means "shining" or "glittering." It's a term Lynn teaches Katie to remind her to see the world as a bright and shiny place, full of beauty and opportunity. At the end of the book, the family moves to California and, when they get to the beach, Katie hears Lynn's voice in the waves shouting "Kira-Kira! Kira-Kira!"

---

53 Cynthia Kadohata, *Kira-Kira* (New York: Antheneum Books for Young Readers, 2004).

For some reason ever since, the voice in my head began repeating "don't sweat the shiny stuff," I also started to think about the younger sister's character development in *Kira-Kira*, and the lessons I could glean from it. Was the point of the story that it took an incredible tragedy for her to realize that her life was valuable and that she should try harder? Or was it the fact that despite her getting all the accolades and achievements her family always wanted for her, all of the "glitters" couldn't bring back what was most important to her—the life of her sister? Maybe the answer was some combination of both…I never got around to rereading the novel. But the story of *Kira-Kira* in tandem with Rick's lecture and the voice in my head all motivated me to think deeply about what was most important to me.

I still needed to find my ultimate concern—a mission or goal that organized and gave meaning to everything that I did. It shouldn't take a rejection from One Medical, a third-place finish at the Los Angeles hackathon, or a divine intervention to push me to take my life more seriously. On the other hand, it also shouldn't require me climbing my way up to the top of the ladder at a prestigious law firm just to realize what's truly important to me and make me shout "Kira-Kira!" into the wind. At this juncture, I had to get it together—and I had to get it together fast because that realization was almost two years overdue.

April was a complete blur. Days bled into one another. The law school sent out a memorandum in the weeks leading up to final exams stating that all classes taken during the spring 2020 semester would be graded on a pass/no pass basis due to the pandemic. When I first heard the news, I was unfazed. I was more concerned about what I was going to do over the summer, considering most companies and law firms had already stopped recruiting and many were even canceling their summer programs and rescinding offers. But, in the days that followed the announcement, I slowly came to the frustrating realization that I had been performing exceptionally well in all of the classes I was enrolled in during the spring and, had the grading system remained numerical, I likely would have seen a significant boost in my cumulative GPA.

I rolled out of bed and made my way to the kitchen. After opening the wooden cabinet closest to the kitchen sink, I proceeded to stare at the loaf of bread sitting in its plastic bag on the second shelf. Outside, I could hear the soft grumbling of a car motor at the stoplight. It was definitely a lot quieter than usual. A lot less chaotic, especially for a weekday. I reached into the plastic bag and pulled out two slices of bread. The top slice had sprouted a patch of what looked like a green, powdery substance, peppered with yellow splotches throughout. Mold. I threw the bread back into the bag and clenched my fists. My eyes grew hot with rage. I tried arching them upward, attempting to contain the moisture that had begun gathering at the corners. I pounded my fists into the bag and molded the loaf through the plastic into a gigantic brown ball. I yelled at the top of my lungs. A groan came from one of my suitemates' room. "Damn," I muttered under my breath. I tossed the moldy ball of wheat into the garbage and sped back to my room. This is exactly what happened to Gabby.

What was I doing? I was crying over some moldy bread. I could get another loaf from Trader Joe's at USC Village. It wasn't the end of the world, but it certainly felt like it. I looked around my room. My laundry was strewn across the floor, papers covered the entire surface area of my desk. I was a mess. All my previous failures that I had tried so desperately to move past suddenly came flooding back. It was a torrential downpour. I sat on the ground at the foot of my bed and closed my eyes, imagining what James or Marty would say if they were right next to me: "It's temporary—it's all temporary, Jesse, and it'll go away. You just gotta go with the flow...be like water...let it go... wait for the rain to pass." As their voices echoed in my head, I could hear the thunder and lightning growing louder. There was no escape. The storm boomed and cracked at an ever-increasing volume, until suddenly I heard a pinging sound.

Ping. My phone vibrated twice, and a banner appeared on the lock screen. I quickly got up to read it. It was a reminder for my Equity, Diversity, and Inclusion (EDI) Committee meeting that was happening via Zoom in five minutes. I had completely forgotten. I quickly clicked the Zoom link to enter the chatroom, and de-selected the video option so the committee members couldn't see what a state of disarray my life was in at the moment. The EDI Committee at Gould is a group of professors, students, and deans who meet every few months to discuss diversity initiatives and other important school policies. I was selected to be a part of it last semester because I was the president of the Student Bar Association's Diversity Committee. It was nice to have a seat at the table and advocate for classmates who were underrepresented minorities and/or who came from diverse backgrounds. Gabby was on the committee too. This week, Andrew Guzman, the dean of Gould, led the conversation about how exams were to be administered throughout the ongoing pandemic.

"Alright, thank you all for joining the session for today," he said with a wide smile. I remembered Dean Guzman from USC's "Law Day"—an annual admitted student event at Gould held in April before the start of 1L. Seeing his face pop up on the Zoom meeting immediately unleashed a wave of nostalgia. As the meeting commenced, my mind began drifting into a reverie. I imagined being back in my senior year of college at Emory again, and USC had just paid for my flight to California. "Going Back To Cali" by Biggie blasted from my headphones. I mumbled through most of the lyrics before chiming in with the only words I knew. "I'm going back to Cali," I rapped aloud, completely off-beat. I made my way to the second to last row of Economy. "I'm going to Los Angeles!" I shouted over the Puff Daddy-produced beat to a woman seated in the aisle across from me. She flinched and replied, "I think we all are."

I got out of my Uber from LAX to USC and looked across the campus in awe, the Romanesque red brick walls towering over me. I stared in admiration at the Rundbogenstil-style arches that decorated the smooth facades of the dormitories. Palm trees danced to the rhythm of USC's Spirit of Troy marching band practicing in the distance. The sky, a cerulean oasis. I couldn't believe it. I was about to become a law student at USC. A Trojan. Everything in my life had led up to this moment. I was full of go. Energized and ready to charge headfirst at whatever came my way. When I finally made my way to "Town & Gown," a building where deans and speakers often hosted events for prospective students and alumni, my jaw dropped. The main room looked like it had been taken straight off a movie set. Golden chandeliers glimmered as they hung from the ceiling. The carpet, a deep red, making anyone who stepped on it into an instant celebrity. Students were given a three-course meal. The dessert? A chocolate mousse with USC's logo emblazoned on top.

I sat at a circular table with eight or nine other accepted students when Dean Guzman walked by and sat down with us. He was dressed sharply in a suit and tie with his signature black-framed glasses. Despite his Hispanic last name, Dean Guzman didn't appear phenotypically Latino. I later learned that his father was Dominican, and his mother Anglo-Saxon. And though he never lived in the Dominican Republic, Dean Guzman spent a fair amount of time there, which he largely attributed to why he has such an affinity for all things international. After he introduced himself, some students asked the dean what his own experience was like in law school. I leaned in to listen to his response, assuming someone of his stature likely breezed through any class he took with flying colors. "Well actually, before I went to law school, I was a PhD candidate in economics at Harvard," he said cheerfully.

He went on to explain how the first year of his PhD program was pretty easy, and he performed fairly well grade-wise. His dream at the time was to become a "topflight economist." But then the second year of the program happened, and things… got complicated. "To provide some context, the level in the PhD program was high to begin with, but because I chose such technically challenging courses, I was placed in the most mathematically competent cohort from within the program. So, I became, roughly speaking, the least mathematically competent person in the most mathematically demanding fields."

While Dean Guzman's math skills were strong, the competition became far stiffer than expected. Being at the bottom of the class was a feeling completely foreign and unknown to Guzman. "It felt like how I imagine it feels to be a Triple A baseball player who is called up to the majors. Suddenly, instead of being among the best on your team, you are a borderline player." Looking back on this memory, I realized that Dean Guzman's analogy hit at the core of exactly how I and those in my remedial criminal law class felt about our collective experience in the law school. Objectively, we all came from strong academic backgrounds and did fairly well as undergraduates. But once we became surrounded by students who were all equally if not more academically capable, it became a completely different playing field.

He continued to explain the context of the class that he had found most challenging, "The term 'corporate finance' was used in economic departments primarily in the context of the pricing of assets. For instance, calculating how much a stock or bond is worth." Fancy investment banks would have teams of economists to help them figure out how to price their assets, and the course was taught by one of the people who invented the field. The course work was often structured in a way that challenged students to develop mathematical proofs to prove how a certain formula works, "A typical thing to do would be to state a formula and show how to develop it through a mathematical proof. So, you'd start with some assumptions that would generate with some mathematical equations, until you got a certain solution that you'd arrive to at the end."

Understanding the steps of the proof, for Guzman, was doable. He knew how to get from one line of the proof to the next. The hard part was the bigger picture. Or "moving from the trees to the forest," as he put it. He explained, "For this math if you really understood it—it's just multivariate calculus. But the problem for me was in application. I could get the proof—I could understand getting from one line to the next. But to be able to write out the entire proof from start to finish? That would take me a very long time." Applying that concept to law school, Dean Guzman likened the proof to reading and understanding a case, "For instance, if you're reading a case, you might understand every section, every fact of the case. But you might not be able to see the big picture—what was the most important part of the case that could be applied to other fact patterns. What was the point of it, essentially?"

He ended up getting a B+ in the class. No one in the PhD program failed because of the curve. But he recalled that his exam was roughly "incoherent" and that his proof "just didn't do the things it was supposed to do." The trauma for him wasn't the grades; however, it was the feeling that he just wasn't smart enough to be the great economist he had always dreamt of becoming. Still, he reminded us that he didn't blame anyone else for his shortcoming. That is, anyone other than himself. "Even with slight objectivity, I didn't deserve any sympathy. I chose those fields and ultimately paid the price."

At the start of his PhD program, Dean Guzman was clear-eyed, gunning for the top position—the highest rung on the ladder in the field of economics. His goal was to influence the debates and the field of economics as a whole. That dream came crashing down when his second year went sideways. As the second year of his PhD program progressed, his outlook on life and his ambitions also became clearer.

Throughout our conversation, it was clear that there were glimmers of doubt shining through even before his final grades came out. "I think at some point I realized that if I wanted to be successful as an economist, I'd essentially say something smart and then someone would take that information to make a decision." In other words, while the economist explains and provides context to whatever problem the bank or corporation is trying to solve, they aren't the ones making the final call at the end of the day. For most people in the field, that wouldn't be a problem. But the dean's goal had always been to incite change. To influence the field from the top down. To have a seat at the table. These were opportunities typically not afforded to the economist he had been aspiring to become. No, making the final call was the job of someone else—the lawyer. "Going to law school, for me, was a pretty liberating decision. My goal was to have a seat at the table and to be the one making decisions. Plus, the law degree—it's relatively short and the job market at the time was reasonably friendly."

Another student chimed in, "So what happened with the PhD program? Did you drop it to pursue your JD?" No, he didn't. Dean Guzman continued to pursue both degrees simultaneously. His second year in the law program, he took a year off to write his dissertation for his PhD. This ended up being one of the dean's most difficult struggles. "So, I took a year off to write my dissertation. The problem was, I was in Toronto with my then-fiancée. And so, what I didn't appreciate was the way the dissertation is written." He explained that typical

PhD candidates spend an exorbitant amount of time staring at a blank sheet of paper, trying to come up with something novel and ingenious to write about.

This was the PhD program's bar exam. The final performance. The elephantine task of creating a dissertation from scratch was enormously difficult on its own, but for Dean Guzman it became even more onerous without the community of the other PhD candidates by his side. "The more typical experience would be: You wake up on a random morning in October, you'd walk to the economics department building where lots of people were doing empirical work, which at the time couldn't be done on a laptop—you had to use computers in the facility. And, you usually spend the next three hours and get nothing done, but at least you can go to lunch with someone else who was in the same boat and feel better about it because at least you were all suffering together. I didn't have any of that because I was in Toronto."

Immediately, Arsh's comment interrupted my stroll down memory lane: *"Thankfully I had an amazing co-founder...just knowing I wasn't alone at that moment of defeat was comforting."* Guzman continued, "A lot of my classmates that year did incredibly well. It was rough; because when you're in the program at Harvard, you're supposed to go to each other's crappy grad school apartments, drink beer, observe that everything sucked and complain about your advisor, I definitely think I would've had a better time if I had that community around me." In the end, Dean Guzman got through it—both the PhD program and law school. After enduring all the struggles that came with both programs, he came out the other side in one piece, although, perhaps, with a slightly bruised ego.

A student raised her hand to ask another question. "Okay, last one and then I gotta run to a meeting," he replied. She blurted out, "Do you think the PhD program helped you at all with law school? Like, did it make 1L easier?" He paused for a moment to think. "So, law school wasn't really easier. It's hard to compare because the two programs were so fundamentally different in terms of intellectual rigor." He analogized the PhD program to a type of brain teaser puzzle that he had played with as a child: "It's like one of those puzzles with a bunch of metal hooks. You know, like the brain teaser game that kids often play with. There's a certain way to solve the puzzle and untangle the hooks. But if you don't know how to do it, you end up just staring at it. That's like the PhD program."

By contrast, he likened law school to a stepladder: "With law school, you know how to get from point A to point B. That doesn't necessarily make it easier because getting up the ladder is still tough. But you can see the light at the end of the tunnel. The program makes clear the concrete and specific steps that you must take in order to become a lawyer." Ultimately, the dean didn't really have an easy answer to the question. The programs were both rigorous and difficult in their own ways. But the one advantage that the law program had was that it paved a clear path to the professional world—a world in which Dean Guzman would be able to make top-down decisions as a respected lawyer. And, although the education he gained from the PhD program was certainly valuable, he ended up appreciating the legal profession a lot more due to the autonomy it afforded. In short, Guzman's ultimate concern was crystal clear: getting a seat at the table.

"So, does that plan work for everyone?" he said as the meeting began to wrap up.

"Any questions? Jesse?" he added inquisitively.

The red carpet of the Town & Gown morphed back into the wood paneled floor of my apartment. I fell out of my seat at the table of admitted students, back into my own chair in front of my desk.

"Yes!" I said reflexively. "That sounds great."

"Okay awesome, thank you all for a productive meeting. Hope you all stay safe," he replied.

I logged out of the meeting, got back into bed, and pulled the sheets over my head.

Maybe the moral of *Kira-Kira* wasn't so literal. Maybe *Kira-Kira* didn't really have anything to do with the accolades, status, and the "shiny stuff" that usually came with achieving some elusive paradigm of being a perfect person like Lynn. And maybe *Kira-Kira* wasn't about seeing the shiny stuff, like hope and opportunity in the world, at all. Not even figuratively.

All this time I saw big law as this bright, shimmery object that was constantly just out of my reach. And I likened those who got offers to work big law jobs or who found success in the legal field, like Dean Guzman, to Lynn. Or "Lynns" (plural). I mean, at school Lynn looked like she had it all together. She was perfect—smart, popular, charismatic. But a closer look would reveal that her life was far from what it appeared on the surface. She and her family were forced to move because their family-owned oriental foods grocery store went out of business, and her father's job earned him almost nothing, forcing him to sleep at the factory between shifts to make more money. Finally, it revealed that she had a terminal illness that ultimately left her emaciated and her family an emotional wreck.

My interpretation of *Kira-Kira* had been so dichotomous— Lynn was perfect, her sister was a failure; Lynn dies, her death inspires her family to see the world in its flashy, gaudy glory. I had the same interpretation of USC and Dean Guzman. When I first walked on campus, it looked like paradise. When Dean Guzman walked by, I thought he had been valedictorian since kindergarten. And with every step he took, glittering particles seemed to descend from the golden chandeliers scintillating above.

Conversely, I had been focusing so intently on Lynn's death— not being able to get a job in big law, losing out on first place at the hackathon, getting the rejection from One Medical. Her death chased me everywhere, haunting me. Stalking me. Draining me. But seeing only light or dark, or life or death in everything defeated the entire purpose of the story. *Kira-Kira* didn't really mean spinning everything going wrong in my life as a positive, forcing myself to see some kind of fake glitter that wasn't really there. And it didn't mean every setback or tragedy should be seen as some kind of life-altering lesson that would suddenly jolt me awake and motivate me to change myself entirely. *Kira-Kira* was about making the most with what I had and seeing the world in all its beautiful, ugly, messy, realistic splendor.

In the weeks following the EDI meeting, I thought intently about my conversations with Dean Guzman, Gabby, Rick, and Arsh. I still did not know for certain whether I would run for SBA President or not. But I knew this—if I were going to throw my hat into the ring, I had to be certain I was doing it for the right reason. And that reason had to be realistic. Becoming SBA President wasn't going to suddenly alter my life or give meaning to everything I did. It wasn't going to immediately make me a better person or bolster my chances of getting an offer from a law firm. Likewise, losing the election wasn't going to send me down a rabbit hole of spiraling grief (unless I let it) or lead me to some divine revelation.

Taking off the proverbial rose-colored glasses, I had to realize that running for SBA President would not solve any of my problems. In fact, if I won, I would be given a whole host of responsibilities that would likely exacerbate my pre-existing issues. Ultimately, I had to be real with myself—I had to tone down the drama, take a hard look at myself in the mirror, and make an objective assessment of what I really sought to gain from the upcoming election.

CHAPTER 14

GIRL ON FIRE

———

*For more information or to make a
gift to PILF, please visit the donations
page at https://giveto.usc.edu/.*

Sitting at my desk at home with my face buried in my computer screen, I quickly scanned the email I was about to send for any spelling errors, mumbling the words aloud: "'Hi, my name is Jesse and I'm running for SBA President because—screw it, I'm just gonna do it." I shrugged and clicked send. It was the first week of May, and the pandemic was going strong. My communication with classmates had become shorter and less frequent. I think all of us were just trying to do our best to get through finals and be done with the semester.

At that point, I didn't have enough stamina in me to give 100 percent of myself toward the election cycle. Of course, I was still going to try—I just knew my body and mind were too exhausted to push full steam ahead. In addition, during the previous year's election, I ran for the Student Bar Association

Secretary and won, so I figured since I had strong name recognition, I would have a good shot at winning the presidency. At least that's what I thought until I found out who my competition was.

During the first week of May, SBA sent out an email to the entire student body: "Good morning, Gould. Your candidates for the 2020-2021 Student Bar Association President are as follows: Mirelle Raza, Danielle Luchetta, and Jesse Wang." Staring at the black text on the screen, my eyes trembled. I slumped back in my seat. "Shit," I cussed to myself. "Shit shit shit." Shit was right. Mirelle and Danielle were absolute titans in the law school. Sure, I was the SBA Secretary and founder of LTA, but people only really knew me as the guy who sent Monday morning announcements to the school each week.

By contrast, Mirelle was the President of the Public Interest Law Foundation, "PILF," a.k.a. the biggest and oldest student organization in USC Gould history, and Danielle was the elected 2L SBA President and had been elected the 1L SBA Representative for our K-O Super Section the previous year. In that moment, there was no doubt in my mind that this would be one of the most monumental and competitive showdowns in Student Bar Association history. All three of us were strong contenders, but I was definitely the underdog.

I knew both Danielle and Mirelle had already strategized the execution of their campaigns. I could just tell, based on the work they had done for the past two years. I knew this was especially true for Mirelle because she had her ultimate concern locked down even before day one of law school. Leaning back in my chair, I reminisced about the first time

I saw Mirelle walk into one of our SBA meetings. She was wearing a grey pantsuit with black shoes and white dress shirt. Her long, wavy brown hair cascaded down, reaching halfway between her neck and waist.

I distinctly remember one signature feature of hers, which was that she spoke slowly and deliberately. Her voice had a certain softness that conveyed a sense of warmth and friendliness, but it also possessed enough fire and energy to remind us she meant business. The topic of the conversation in that meeting was about PILF funds and how SBA could help with achieving the organization's goal amount. Historically, PILF had provided a set number of summer stipends to certain first year law students interested in working in public interest positions. Students were selected based on a written application, completion of twenty-five hours of pro bono work, and an interview with the PILF alumni.

However, as more students became involved in public interest work, the competition for obtaining the PILF grants gradually became steeper. By the end of the 2019 spring semester, the number of students and the funds needed to cover living expenses greatly surpassed the amount of funds PILF had available for grants. In a last-ditch effort to cover everyone's expenses, PILF asked Dean Guzman and Gould for $40,000 to support the additional students. Dean Guzman approved the request, but even with the additional funding there was still not enough to provide grants for every student that applied.

On top of that, Dean Guzman reminded the executive board, including Mirelle, that a similar occurrence could not happen again. The law school couldn't afford to simply fork over an additional $40,000 every year, and PILF had to develop a plan to support summer grants through PILF's own fundraising moving forward. That was when Mirelle knew it was go time. From that point onward, she was on a mission to make sure PILF would never have to turn down another student who wanted to work for a good cause, and she was determined to make it happen.

Despite her short five-foot-three stature, Mirelle always delivered her points with such confidence and poise that it felt like she was towering over us on an invisible podium. While she wasn't a member of SBA, she was still a giant among us when she attended our meetings to discuss developments about PILF. When she attended her first SBA meeting after she was appointed president, it was a surprise to everyone that, at the time, she had only been running the organization for a couple of months and possessed zero background in business administration. Yet, from the get-go, she had been hustling hard—networking with donors, organizing fundraisers, meeting with the law school deans, and so on. She was that good. And, though she led with a strong sense of egalitarianism, everyone acknowledged and respected her as the commander-in-chief. She was, without a doubt, the boss. The top dog. And, perhaps, that was the role that came most naturally to her, because she handled it with such ease.

What made Mirelle different and a true leader, though, at least from my perspective, was her stoicism. She was always fairly reserved and never openly expressed any extreme emotion. No—Mirelle was too focused on getting results to allow emotions to get the best of her. In fact, her favorite movie character was Katniss Everdeen from *The Hunger Games Trilogy* because her personality resonated with her; both were courageous, cool-headed introverts.[54] And that's what scared me. She was effective—very effective. People looked up to her. She was the girl on fire, and she had accomplished some pretty significant achievements to back that title up.

After that initial SBA meeting, Mirelle and I had a long conversation over lunch by the fountain outside of the law school. She told me about how she first realized her passion for public interest work while she was still an undergraduate at Santa Clara University. As a women's & gender studies and sociology double major, she discovered the importance of advocacy and using her voice. Before law school, she landed two internships that shaped her future career—the first was at Santa Clara County's Office of Women's Policy, and the second was in Santa Clara County's District Attorney's Office in the Victim Services Unit. What she learned through both positions is the importance of having direct service experience when participating in policy work, to ensure that policies not only look good on paper but also are productive in practice.

Additionally, it became clear how important it was to have community members at the table who can advocate for themselves. Mirelle used California Assembly Bill 1997 as an example as the bill required that children be placed in a family-like setting within ten days of entering a shelter-care facility or group home.[55] While this policy is a positive step

---

54 Sabaa Tahir, "Katniss Everdeen Is My Hero," *New York Times*, October 18, 2018.
55 "Assembly Bill No. 1997 CHAPTER 612," California Legislative Information, accessed September 13, 2020.

for reducing the number of children in non-family settings, it became problematic for a subset of children within this population that had been victims of human trafficking. This population is referred to as "commercially sexually exploited children" or "CSEC."[56]

CSEC have specialized needs that often require long-term placements in shelters that provide wrap-around services. Mirelle noted this was an example where community members and advocates working with policy makers could have created a solution that considered the needs of CSEC as well. In addition, as a woman of color, Mirelle was driven to be a champion for other people of color and marginalized populations and advocate alongside her community members. She was driven, the moment she stepped through the front doors of Gould, to make a difference.

Still, working in public interest wasn't always in the cards for Mirelle—at least, not immediately. She explained that during her first year out of college, she accepted a sales associate position for a company that had nothing to do with her major or her previous internships in women's advocacy. She took it because she had loans to pay off and needed to support herself financially. Mirelle quickly discovered that the cost of working a job that fundamentally misaligned with her core beliefs was a far greater burden to carry than she had anticipated.

Not only did she hate her job, which involved making a great deal of unsolicited calls to potential customers (i.e. cold

56 "Commercial Sexual Exploitation of Children (CSEC)," County Welfare Directors Association of California, accessed September 12, 2020.

calling), she also stopped working out and maintaining a healthy diet. The combination of unhealthy behaviors in tandem with an overwhelming feeling of profound disappointment led Mirelle to become depressed: "I was so unfulfilled because I felt like I was just bothering people all day by calling them about a product they just didn't care about when all I really wanted to do was to help people." It wasn't until she finally summoned the strength to leave her job that she was able to finally climb out of that dark hole and return to what made her feel alive—public interest.

On the bright side, though, Mirelle explained that the experience, while miserable, was also an eye-opener. It was the sales job that not only motivated Mirelle to attend law school, but also made her realize her ultimate concern—advocating for vulnerable populations and survivors of sexual violence. This was a purpose that was so intrinsic and necessary to her, that working a job that prevented her from pursuing it, regardless of how much it paid, would not satisfy her.

That year-long stint of pure agony helped Mirelle realize, decisively, that she personally could not go the big law route. The money simply wasn't worth her mental and physical well-being, "I just knew that if I ended up at one of those larger firms, it would be like my experience in sales all over again. And this is not by any means me judging those who do choose the big law route—it's a very respectable job, and I'm sure people enjoy it. It's just not for me, personally. Also, my sales experience really highlighted how important my physical health is, and it's something I can't sacrifice again."

In addition to the mental and emotional toll the sales job had on Mirelle, she also suffered from a serious medical ailment. Diagnosed with an autoimmune disease in college, the stress of the sales job led to a flare up, which landed her in the hospital. She explained that frequently with an autoimmune disease, doctors have no idea what's going on, so while they try their best to figure out which medication will work, patients are put on harsh steroids to control the disease: "It really pushed me to the limits physically, and I lost a ton of muscle. But the good news was, it gave me the kick in the butt that I needed." When Mirelle got out of the hospital, she immediately applied for the job at the DA's office and pushed herself physically to get back to playing rugby.

Four months after the hospital scare, Mirelle was playing in the USA Club Rugby National Championship game with her teammates on Life West Gladiatrix. And they won. She related how rugby changed her life: "I think rugby helped me both physically and emotionally because it allowed me to be part of a community that supported me and pushed me. That was really important especially in my first year out of college." Mirelle explained that being part of a rugby team reminded her of how important community was to her. When she was working in sales, she stopped seeing a lot of her friends from college despite living close to them. She was keeping the hard times to herself and the isolation ate away at her: "I learned that lesson and that's why, when I have a hard moment, day, or week during law school, I know to lean on my community and focus on the reasons I'm here. And when I do that, I find success."

Mirelle's commitment to the public interest community at Gould helped to remind her time and time again why she wanted to become a lawyer in the first place. Interacting with like-minded peers gave her energy; they invigorated and inspired her to keep pushing to help as many people as possible. PILF was like Mirelle's new rugby team, and the away team was structural inequality and poverty. And, while PILF may not have won a national championship game, they did achieve something far more valuable: justice. She explained, "As part of my pro bono work this year, we helped a human trafficking client get a T-Visa after ten years of hiding. It was such an amazing feeling to watch the joy and relief she had when signing those papers. You almost can't describe how incredible the moment was for us. It was bigger than any championship."

I closed out of the email from SBA and thought about how much PILF had accomplished since my conversation with Mirelle that day by the water fountain. Since then, PILF doubled its introductory meeting attendance from the previous year, successfully hosted its annual PILF auction event to fund summer grants and received a $2 million estate endowment from Mrs. Barbara Bice—the wife of one of Gould's most esteemed tort professors and former dean of the law school, Professor Scott Bice. PILF was renamed in Mrs. Bice's honor and is now known as The Barbara F. Bice Public Interest Law Foundation.

Lastly, and most importantly, was Mirelle's magnum opus— her crowning achievement as PILF President. Following months of negotiations between the PILF executive board and Dean Guzman, the school announced a landmark commitment: Beginning in the summer of 2020, every first- and second-year law student who completed the application requirements and was participating in qualified public interest work would receive a summer grant. As a result, in 2020, PILF distributed a record-breaking thirty-two summer public interest grants, in addition to seven 2L bonuses and seven 3L bar stipends. Altogether, Gould and PILF provided a total of $195,000 to the public interest students.

Still on my computer, I listlessly scrolled through my news feed for a few moments before opening a word document to jot down my thoughts. What could I take away from Mirelle's story that could help me with my own campaign? How could the discovery of her ultimate concern help me find mine? After typing out some of the key points Mirelle had made during our conversation, I had a revelation: The way Mirelle found her ultimate concern was by aligning three key factors, (1) interest, (2) purpose, and (3) career. First, she cultivated her interest through women's & gender studies at Santa Clara. This interest in women's rights led her to find her purpose—advocating for women of color and vulnerable populations. Finally, she had to find an avenue to invest in both her interest and purpose professionally, which led her to her internship at the DA's office and, subsequently, law school to become a lawyer.

I thought deeply about what I was interested in. I've always enjoyed being creative and my biggest wins, such as founding LTA and coming up with the concept for MentalBrief, all stemmed from that. In terms of my purpose, mental health within the legal community was an extremely important cause for me personally. I was especially passionate about developing technology to make mental health services more accessible to lawyers. *"That was easy. Two down, and one to go,"* I thought to myself.

The final prong was career. How could becoming the SBA President help me cultivate my creativity and mental health advocacy? That was the key question. I stared at the open document for the next half hour. How could I, as SBA President, use my creativity to bring counselors to the law school? The idea seemed easier in my head. I mean, just invent an app for law students to use, like MentalBrief, except for law school, right? But how would that work...who would develop it and where would I get the money to create it. Also, even if we were to get a fully functioning app, would people use it, given TeleHealth's poor reputation when it comes to user privacy and risk protection?[57]

After failing to come up with a single concrete idea, I got up from my desk and headed to the kitchen to brew some coffee. As the Keurig machine hummed and sputtered out the black liquid into my mug, I shook my head and muttered aloud, "This is going to be a bloodbath."

---

57 Timothy M. Hale and Joseph C. Kvedar, "Privacy and Security Concerns in Telehealth," *AMA Journal of Ethics*, Vol. 2 (2014): 216-221.

CHAPTER 15

LITTLE ITALY

—

"Coo...coo...," a mourning dove cried outside my window. Stretching its wings a few times, it cocked its head from side to side before abruptly flying away. I peered through the dusty plexiglass sipping my coffee and saw a single black feather lying on the windowsill where the bird had been perched. *"How appropriate,"* I thought to myself. I read a book a while back called *The Black Swan* by Nassim Nicholas Taleb.[58] The black swan theory is basically a metaphor for an event that seemingly comes out of nowhere and has a major impact on the world.[59] Usually the event is completely unpredictable, but inappropriately rationalized in hindsight.[60] What I liked about the book specifically was that Taleb never pretended he could foresee unpredictable events or tried to teach us how. His main purpose was to help readers cultivate a sense of robustness or, in his words, "antifragility"—the ability to thrive and actually become stronger in moments of volatility and shock. Some examples include the Hydra, a creature

---

58 Nassim Nicholas Taleb, *The Black Swan: The Impact of the Highly Improbable* (New York: Random House, 2007).

59 Ibid.

60 Ibid.

that grows back stronger with two heads when one is cut off, and hypertrophy, a process in which muscles increase in size when damaged from working out.[61] By becoming more antifragile, we would be less susceptible to black swan events and, in fact, welcome their occurrence.

Taleb provided many great principles for cultivating antifragility, but the three that stood out to me the most were:

1. Respect the old, keeping an eye out for habits and rules that have withstood the test of time,
2. Resist the urge to suppress randomness, and
3. Keep your options open—remain afloat by trying many different things and maintaining an open mind while being careful to avoid total failure.[62]

Placing my coffee mug on the desk beside me, I climbed back into bed and thought about what Danielle might have planned for her campaign. I thought back to when I first met her at orientation. I remembered she was the girl with green eyes and olive-toned skin. Typically sporting round glasses and a high ponytail, she'd spend countless hours in the law library pouring over materials, relentlessly plugging away at her assignments. If she wasn't busy working on her own assignments, she was hard at work helping classmates outline or explaining to them difficult civil procedure concepts. She was the epitome of a team player. Danielle's mindset had always been set on putting the needs of those within her community first.

61 Buster Benson, "Live Like a Hydra: Thoughts on How to Get Stronger When Things are Chaotic," Medium, August 24, 2013.
62 Ibid.

Danielle and I often chatted before our legal writing class about miscellaneous topics ranging from our favorite movies to places we wanted to travel. I'd always wanted to go to Italy and hearing her describe the Roman architecture and waterfronts of Crema and Bergamo helped me imagine myself in paradise instead of law school. At least for a few fleeting moments. She spoke to me about how close she was with her family in Italy and that, while she couldn't speak Italian herself, she could speak Spanish to them whenever she visited. I could tell from her story and from learning her background as a middle child from a big Italian family, that Danielle's heart and identity, in large part, lay within the home. Danielle was someone driven to make connections and build a community that she could call her home. Her ability to understand and connect with others was her most valuable asset, but that also meant it came with some tough choices.

Before law school, Danielle studied business and film at Chapman University in Orange, California. She was dead set on becoming an entertainment lawyer and breaking into the film industry. So, after graduating, Danielle secured a job on the corporate communications team at Twentieth Century Fox. And she loved it.

Working at Fox brought Danielle a deep sense of joy. She loved working in film, and her entire team could feel her passion. It wasn't long before her roles and responsibilities were increased and, by the end of 2018, Danielle had been promoted three times, from assistant to associate manager. But what made Danielle love Fox the most wasn't so much related to the professional aspects, as much as it was the emotional and personal connections she made. "No matter what I was doing, I realized it was the people at Fox who kept me there so long. They were my family and, to this day, there's no divide in that sense. They'll always be a part of my life no matter what," she explained. She told me that even now, two years into law school, she continues to attend her coworkers' weddings, baby showers, and other get-togethers. Fox was her home, and her coworkers were her family. And whenever Danielle built a home, a piece of her always remained there. No matter what.

However, the unfortunate reality was that the stronger the emotional attachment became, the harder it was for Danielle to pursue her own individual dreams. She had entered her role at Fox with the intent of becoming an entertainment lawyer. It was meant to be a steppingstone, and it was time to get off it, regardless of how much joy it gave her. For Danielle, becoming a lawyer was inevitable, and she knew that it had something to do with her selfless nature. After all, serving as someone's attorney was an enormous responsibility and required a great deal of dedication and sacrifice. The lawyer was, first and foremost, the client's advisor and advocate— someone who could be trusted and who defended that trust at all costs. It was the perfect role for her. Despite all this, Danielle ended up postponing the decision time and time again. Even after applying and getting accepted to USC, Danielle was on the fence. At least she was until the decision was made for her.

One day, Danielle walked into Fox and saw her coworkers sitting around a table in silence. It had been announced earlier that morning that Fox was going to be merged with Disney, and a large portion of the Fox employees would be laid off as part of the change in management. Danielle never went into detail about how she personally felt about the merger or how it impacted her coworkers. But given how close she was with her Fox "family," it likely wasn't one of her fonder memories. She told me. "It was a really big shift. And, at the time, I knew I wanted to go to law school, but I also really loved working in film. So, when the merger was announced, it was like the universe pushing me out of my safety zone and encouraging me to apply."

Danielle was not someone who struck me as a risk-taker. Actually, she was probably one of the most meticulous, rule-abiding persons I'd ever known. Her favorite classes were Civil Procedure and Constitutional Law, likely because both had a lot of rules. So, taking the leap of faith and leaving Fox was certainly not a walk in the park for her. She explained, "Your twenties are such a defining decade. And for most of my twenties up until that point, I had been going with the flow. It was what I was used to. It was safe. Like home." Nevertheless, after the initial shock of the merger, Danielle decided to swim against the current and apply for law school. Once she got her acceptance letter to USC, she was absolutely stoked and ready to make the most of it.

From the first day of 1L year, Danielle was on a mission—to create a new home. A Trojan home with a new family—her classmates. She ran for our Super Section's 1L representative Student Bar Association position and won soundly, which gave her greater access to helping her peers. Throughout her time as a 1L rep, Danielle balanced the academic rigors of 1L year with planning and organizing events on behalf of her classmates, getting to know everyone, and advocating for their needs behind the scenes. "For 1L SBA members, we were able to help out so much by advocating for our peers and even just being present for people when someone needed to listen or talk things through."

Listening. That was one of Danielle's best skills. And she used it profusely throughout her time on SBA. "We go through 1L and it's all the doctrinal classes plus legal writing plus trying to find a summer job when you just finished the hardest semester of your life. It's a difficult time for everyone. And so, sometimes if you can be there for someone else and just listen to them voice how they're feeling—simply being present is such a powerful thing."

But Danielle's mission didn't stop there. At the end of her 1L year, she ran for 2L Class President and won that election as well. That role opened up and expanded Danielle's reach and her ability to connect with the entire 2L class, as opposed to just our Super Section—an opportunity she did not take for granted. Throughout our 2L year, Danielle worked relentlessly, helping classmates (both 1Ls and 2Ls) find connections and job opportunities. During the spring semester, she even organized an "OCI & Beyond" event with the 2L Class Vice President to help 1Ls get a better understanding of the OCI process. "A lot of times, USC does a phenomenal job focusing on certain aspects of OCI, but I think the goal of 'OCI & Beyond' was to make sure that in addition to networking with firms, students also had the opportunity to network with each other. A lot of people go to USC because of the Trojan alumni network and a big part of that is having peers that you go to school with be there for you and support you!"

"OCI & Beyond" was a manifestation of Danielle's drive to establish a home at USC and a sense of belonging for herself as well as for her classmates. And through speaking with countless classmates and alumni from USC, Danielle was able to attract a massive turnout at her event from a host of different legal industries. "Most of the alumni were from big law firms, but we also had a lot of mid-sized and small firm attorneys from USC as well! So many students want different things, and I think having an event that connects people from within the USC community is so important." Danielle's profound belief in her network and family eventually led her to one of her biggest accomplishments in law school: landing a job at a big law firm.

The summer before her 2L year, Danielle was working for a judge in Orange County, who was also a USC law graduate, when Gould's Career Services reached out to see if she'd like to schedule a mock interview with a USC alum. She jumped at the opportunity to meet someone from within the Trojan Network and the connection she felt when they finally met was instant. "I signed up for the interview back in August and almost forgot about it until it came around in December. And when we finally met, it felt like a great rapport immediately." One reason the conversation flowed so naturally was Danielle's preparation; she had come up with several questions specifically tailored to the firm the alum was from, which demonstrated her genuine interest, "I asked a ton of questions, which I think made our dialogue a lot more engaging. And it wasn't forced at all—I was actually really excited. I wanted to know who worked at the firm, what were the most popular practice groups, and what kinds of pro bono opportunities they had."

She was also honest about her interests, which added to her genuineness, "I was very honest about the fact that while I worked in entertainment for so long, I didn't want to just focus on one industry. I was very open about that because I really want to try every opportunity when it comes to practicing law." As a result, the interviewer was so impressed that she invited Danielle back for a screener interview for the firm, which ultimately led to an offer. Reflecting upon her experience, Danielle told me her story was "kind of wild" because it really epitomized the strength of the Trojan network. And while she acknowledged that many people, especially incoming Gould students, may be skeptical of how strong the network is or whether it lives up to the hype, her experience was a testament to its strength and ability to provide students with meaningful, and ultimately fruitful, professional opportunities.

Still lying in bed, I reached over to open the window beside me and picked up the black feather the pigeon had left behind earlier. Examining it carefully, I took a picture of it with my phone and saved it as my lock screen background. I laid back down and thought about the three tips Taleb had mentioned about becoming antifragile and how Danielle's story embodied them. The first was "respect the old." In other words, keep an eye out for basic principles and rules that have stood the test of time.

For Danielle, that tip was manifest in her respect for her family's classic Italian American values—namely her selflessness and devotion to community. The age-old rule of putting family first was a value that ran through her blood and one that followed her throughout her time at Fox. And, while not her primary focus, it definitely led her to a great deal of success and several promotions. By constantly investing in her relationships with coworkers and treating them like family, Danielle made life-long friends who supported and empowered her. But then, the black swan swooped in and threatened to destabilize everything she had worked so hard to establish.

Nobody foresaw the merger with Disney. It came completely out of left field and left so many of her coworkers reeling. That's when Danielle embodied Taleb's second point, by resisting the urge to suppress randomness. Instead of staying with Disney and seeing if she could keep the position she spent years to attain, she decided to take the plunge. She had known all along she wanted to become a lawyer, and so, instead of fighting the volatility and trying to staple herself to the ground, she jumped. And she stuck her landing. As a law student, she flourished. Still respecting and following the old, she treated her classmates like family and maintained her selfless nature, leading her to win two consecutive SBA elections.

Law school was also the time when Taleb's third tip came into play. After re-establishing a sense of security within the Gould community, Danielle took smaller, more controlled risks to keep her options open. Networking with countless USC alumni, ranging from big law associates to judges, Danielle made a point not to confine herself to one area of law. She was open to all of them and stayed away from putting all her eggs into one basket. It was this open-mindedness and candor about her mindset that struck a chord with the recruiter, which eventually landed her the offer at her dream law firm.

In the end, Danielle demonstrated that she was antifragile. It wasn't that she was fearless or immune to anxiety over uncertainty—in fact, Danielle was one of the more risk-averse people I knew in law school. No—Danielle's antifragility stemmed from her ability to balance the old and the new. By taking calculated risks and keeping an open mind while maintaining a sturdy backbone from her Italian upbringing, Danielle cultivated the crucial skill of being able to blossom, while others would wither, amid adversity.

Now, it was time for me to face my own black swan. It was here. Preening itself in front of me. Mockingly. Cocking its head from side to side, knowing that I was terrified. But I had to be strong; or rather, I had to be antifragile—like Danielle— and prosper in the face of this completely unforeseen election cycle. As the bird glared at me with its cold, beady eyes, I stared back. I trembled in fear but was ready to tackle it with everything I had.

CONCLUSION

THE UNDERDOG

———

It was pitch black. I stood still inside the empty room. I could hear whispering sounds coming from all around me. As they grew louder, I listened intently to what they were saying:

"Almost, Jesse, almost gifted..."

"Maybe success just wasn't within your jurisdiction..."

"Who are you, and what do *you* want to do in this lifetime?"

I screamed back, "Shut up! Shut up! Shut up! I know who I am! I know what I'm going to do! I'll show you! I will show you!"

A trap door opened beneath me. The room swallowed me whole. Falling into the dark abyss, I continued to scream, "I will show you! I swear to God, I will show you! I have that fire inside me!" I violently kicked my left foot into the wall beside me, jolting myself awake. I had fallen asleep. Golden slivers of light glimmered between the cracks of the blinds, casting long strands of luster onto the hardwood floor. Had I slept through the entire night? I glanced at my watch. It was five in the morning. Class wouldn't start for another four hours, so I had some time to kill.

After putting on a hospital mask, I made my way down the staircase and out the front door of my apartment. The streets were relatively barren, save for a few cars at the stoplight. Feeling the warmth of the hot Los Angeles sun beating down on me was comforting. In the midst of all of the chaos in the world, it was the one thing that remained consistent. I put on my headphones as I made my way down Exposition Boulevard and across the street toward the USC campus.

"Party for Me" by Jhene Aiko came on. The song opened with the sound of wind chimes and crashing waves before the beat came triumphantly booming through, supported by Jhene's silky vocals. I looked up. Not a cloud in the sky.

As the wind blew past me, I thought about everything I had experienced in the past two years. About the stories I heard and the people I met. I'd changed so much since I first stepped on campus back in 2018. Back then, I thought I had it all figured out–I'd study and grind as hard as I could, get top grades, receive an offer from a big law firm, and make a ton of money. But that ambition was so short-sighted and naive. It completely failed to consider the possibility of failure—which was exactly what happened. Looking back, I realized how grateful and fortunate I was to have met the people who would end up teaching me the true worth of my law school experience.

Marty taught me to be myself. Relentlessly. To be creative and not put too much emphasis on what everyone else thought was valuable or their opinions of me. Gabby taught me to see myself as a person deserving of a full and happy life and separate identity from my accomplishments. Professor Moini taught me to invest in my community and to connect with like-minded individuals who would, in turn, invest back in me. Arsh taught me to appreciate the small wins because they were crucial to building confidence and momentum. Mirelle taught me to have a purpose. A mission. Because if my values didn't align with my work, then, in all likelihood, I'd end up miserable and depressed. Professor Rich taught me to take risks and not to worry too much about being perfect. James taught me to let go of the things I couldn't control because they would only lead to more stress and anxiety. Rick taught me not to sweat the prestige and accolades that came with good grades and working at a name-brand law firm. Chinelo taught me to view myself holistically and to not focus too much on one specific narrative about who I was. Adam taught me to establish healthy work-life boundaries because failing to do so would inevitably lead to burnout. Danielle taught me the virtue of balancing old and new—keeping an open mind and taking small risks, while abiding by age-old principles. And lastly, Dean Guzman taught me to view life realistically because while people may seem perfect on the outside, deep down they've faced obstacles and hardships that can't be seen from the surface.

A warm breeze brushed past my face. I made my way past Leavey Library and through the quadrangle. Two dogs were play wrestling one another in the grass as their owners supervised under the shade of a nearby oak tree. I thought intently about what all my peers had in common. What was the central nexus that wove all their experiences together into a cohesive whole? I mean, they all overcame varying degrees of hardships.

They each demonstrated immense resilience, and many of them had a clear ultimate concern that helped them persevere through some pretty unfortunate moments in their lives. Times when the odds were stacked against them. I guess they were all, in a way, the underdogs. The people who had been counted out—those who fell from grace and had to climb their way back to realize what true success really meant to them. They each fought their way through mental health episodes, despondency, depression, anxiety, and hopelessness. I made it to the edge of campus and jogged in place for a moment before turning back around.

Still brainstorming what my campaign's message would be, I tried to piece together the palette of stories I had heard about mental health, antifragility, grit, black swans, like-minded people, etc. It all seemed like a hodge-podge of randomness—a Jackson Pollock mural.

After making it back to my apartment, I sat down at my desk and started to write down everything that came to mind. I just had to get everything out of my head. It didn't matter if it was word vomit at that point—I just wanted something concrete and visual. I knew each of my peers' individual lessons and stories; now it was time to apply them.

Remembering Danielle's lesson on antifragility, I knew I had to start with the old. Who were the individuals who had been in the legal world the longest and whose lessons withstood the test of time? Dean Guzman and Rick Merrill both came to mind. Their lessons primarily had to do with how people often put too much emphasis on grades and prestige, both of which were not necessarily the best indicators of success, or even happiness. So, what if my campaign platform focused on changing the grading system at Gould?

I opened my laptop and logged onto the law portal to view the student handbook's grading policy. I knew classes were graded numerically and switching to a credit/no credit system would likely be out of the question, but I thought perhaps it'd be possible to change the policy on how classes were curved.

One of the sections discussed grading adjustments for small courses and stipulated that courses with twelve or fewer students enrolled for a numeric grade may use the grade normalization program with the standard target mean or without the normalization program provided that the resulting mean grade for the class exceeds the course's target mean grade by no more than 0.2 or falls below it by more than 0.1. In other words, there was still a possibility for courses with twelve or fewer students to be curved. I thought that was ridiculous. I took an elective in the fall semester with three students. What if the professor had chosen to curve that class normally? We would have all received the median, or even below median grade, regardless of how well we performed. I jotted down a few thoughts and continued brainstorming.

Mental health was another recurring theme. Immediately, I felt the gut-punch of the hackathon fiasco that left me reeling for weeks. I thought about Mirelle in her cubicle, placing her head in her lap for a moment of reprieve, as the dial tone rang after another failed cold-call with a disinterested customer. I imagined Marty lying motionless in his bed, staring numbly at the ceiling of his San Francisco apartment after being fired from the dream start-up he had moved across the country to work for. I had to do something about the state of mental health at Gould. How could I provide my peers with better access to mental health services, without breaking the bank? I scribbled something down and chewed on my pencil, pondering a third angle for my campaign.

Grades and mental health were important, but they weren't necessarily the most attractive or fun topics to discuss. The last thing I wanted people to think was that I was too serious. More importantly, though, those two focuses didn't fully encapsulate what I had learned. There was still a big chunk missing—a more human component. A "people" component. No—it had to be more specific than that. A "like-minded" people component. I thought about what Professor Moini, Arsh, and Danielle had emphasized about finding a community and how meeting people that matched their outlook on life had helped them the most. I pictured a downtrodden Arsh calling up the co-founder of the start-up after coming to the stark reality that their company would never be what they had hoped. I imagined him hanging up his phone after their conversation had ended and heaving a heavy sigh of both exhaustion and relief, knowing that the pain of failure was so much duller because he wasn't alone in it.

Putting down my pencil, I lifted the sheet of paper up to the window to read it more clearly. At the top, in all caps, read: "JESSE'S VISION AS SBA PRESIDENT." Underneath it was the three initiatives I would spearhead as SBA President:

"INITIATIVE #1: FIGHT FOR A FAIRER CURVE."

It was no secret that the law school grading curve was fundamentally unfair and, to some extent, arbitrary. The first major step I planned to take was to draft a memorandum to the deans of the law school advocating that classes with fewer than thirty students be mandatorily uncurved. That way, more people would be able to receive grades that accurately matched their performance in the class, and fewer students would be discouraged due to receiving marks that were lower than what they deserved simply due to the grading distribution policy.

"INITIATIVE #2: MAKE MENTAL HEALTH A PRIORITY."

After hearing so many stories of classmates and alumni who had experienced depression during law school and weren't able to get the help they needed due to their busy schedules, I knew this had to be one of my top concerns. While MentalBrief wasn't a viable product yet, there were other mental health and virtual therapy apps readily available on the market. My second priority would be to persuade the law school to purchase a license on behalf of the student body to get free access to the virtual therapy app, Talkspace. Other schools, such as Williams College, had already partnered with the company, and, considering Gould had considerably fewer students, this was certainly a viable option.[63]

---

63 "University Partnership with Williams College Enrolled Students Will Have Ongoing, No-cost Access to Licensed Therapists Through Talkspace Online Therapy," Cision: PR Newswire, accessed September 15, 2020.

"INITIATIVE #3: SLICE & PINT."

The last point I wanted to emphasize was the importance of networking. Sure, the law school had numerous formal networking events and firm receptions, but there had never been an informal networking event, where individuals from multiple areas of law could converse in a more relaxed, casual setting. That was where "Slice & Pint" came into play. Back at Emory, there was a restaurant called "Slice & Pint" right next to campus, where students would go to grab pizza or drink with friends. I wanted to bring that atmosphere of Southern comfort and ease to law school. So, my third initiative would be to establish a bi-weekly informal networking event where students, alumni, professors, and firm recruiters could socialize and unwind after a stressful week of reading torts or wrapping up a case assignment.

Now, it was time to put it all together. I had to figure out how these three initiatives: grades, mental health, and networking, would weave together into one, cohesive campaign. Staring at the sheet of paper, I circled each of the tactics and drew lines between them. Mental health and grades were definitely connected. I knew this firsthand—the lower my grades were, the worse my mental health became. Then, there was networking. Networking and mental health aligned because the more like-minded and supportive people I had around, the more secure I felt. But when my mental health and grades were lower, the fewer opportunities I had to network, because firms didn't want to talk to students with lower GPAs. It kind of seemed like those at the bottom of the class were more likely to be more depressed, have fewer job opportunities, and feel lonelier and more isolated as a result.

A lightbulb flashed above my head. I knew how they all tied together. I finally knew what my ultimate concern was. I drew an even larger circle around all three of the points. Then, I scribbled a pair of ears, two eyes, a few spots, and a tongue. The crudely drawn face of a dog looked back at me from the page. The goal that got me out of bed every morning—that elusive target I should have known before I even came to law school—was staring me right in the face.

My ultimate concern was fighting for the underdog. I was fighting for those who felt lost, because they had come out of their first year of law school with grades that didn't match how hard they worked or how intelligent they truly were. I was fighting for those who felt hopeless because they were ashamed of being depressed and afraid to seek the professional help they desperately needed to get better. Most importantly, I was fighting for the despondent law students—those who, after desperately trying to improve their grades or network with law firms to no avail, were on the verge of calling it quits. These people were the underdogs, and I was one of them.

All my life I had been so ashamed of being the underdog. Yet I realized, in that moment, the value and strength that the label had brought me. Now, it was time for me to use that to lift up the other underdogs in my class. Underneath "JESSE'S VISION" I wrote in all-caps: "FIGHTING FOR THE UNDERDOGS."

I turned on my laptop and opened up Canva to start designing my campaign flyer. As my eyes glided over the color palette for the flyer background, I pulled out my phone and selected a random podcast on my playlist to play aloud. A familiar voice reverberated through my headset. In a sooth-ing tone, her voice chassed over the words I had heard over a year ago. I closed my eyes and envisioned myself sitting in my dark bedroom back home in Audubon. I pictured the frozen oasis just outside my window, casting a white glow through the gossamer curtains. The weight of my peak sadness from that time lay heavily on my shoulders, like a gargoyle that had just swooped down from my darkest, most repressed memories and chosen me as its perch.

Her bright voice echoed and projected through the audito-rium in the recording: "One way to think about grit is to consider what grit isn't. Grit isn't talent. Grit isn't luck. Grit isn't how intensely, for the moment, you want something. Instead, grit is about having what some researchers call an 'ultimate concern'–a goal you care about so much that it organizes and gives meaning to almost everything you do. And grit is holding steadfast to that goal. Even when you fall down. Even when you screw up. Even when prog-ress toward that goal is halting or slow."[64] Angela Duck-worth concluded her lecture, and the audience erupted with applause.

Opening my eyes, I paused the recording and felt a wave of relief mixed with a strong tinge of anxiety. Angela's words, as always, struck home. But listening to the podcast again brought with it the bitter memories associated with the win-ter of 1L year. Dark tendrils placed themselves carefully back onto the indents of the scars on my psyche, remnants of the

---

64   Angela Duckworth, "FAQ: What is Grit?" Angela Duckworth, accessed
       September 15, 2020.

emotional wounds inflicted just a year prior. The knots of stress between my shoulder blades tensed and pulled at the muscle underneath. I rolled my neck in a circular motion, trying desperately to loosen the strain.

I opened the drawer beneath my desk and pulled out a black plastic Bic lighter and a grey box. Making my way outside to the porch of my apartment, I unwrapped the plastic seal on the box, revealing twenty tubes of paper, brown leaves tucked snugly within each. I slid one out of the box and held it in my mouth, while lifting the lighter up close. The flame canal hovered just a few centimeters away from the tip of the white paper tube clenched between my teeth. I lifted my thumb to the steel spur and paused.

I took a deep breath.

A warm breeze blew past, as I stood still for a few moments. Immediately, I ran into the kitchen, threw all twenty cigarettes into the trash, and ran back into my room, slamming the door behind me.

"No more," I thought to myself.

No more succumbing to bad habits. No more indulging negative self-talk. No more feeling bad for myself, yet not doing anything about it. No more mourning bad grades.

The reality was, I was going to fail. In fact, I was going to fail over and over again, no matter how hard I tried to prevent it. But with over a year's worth of retrospection, I knew better, and I had a game plan.

I tapped the touchpad of my laptop and re-entered Canva to continue designing my flyer. Placing my fingers on the black keys of my laptop, I typed out a short sentence under the main title. In bolded letters, the text read: "We might be the underdogs, but it's not over until we say it is."

APPENDIX

CHAPTER 1

Angela Duckworth. "About Angela." Accessed September 3, 2020. https://angeladuckworth.com/about-angela/.

Fessler, Leah. "'You're No Genius': Her Father's Shutdowns Made Angela Duckworth a World Expert on Grit." Quartz, March 26, 2018. https://qz.com/work/1233940/angela-duckworth-explains-grit-is-the-key-to-success-and-self-confidence/.

TED, "Grit: The Power of Passion and Perseverance," May 9, 2013, video, 6:12. https://www.youtube.com/watch?v=H14bBulu-wB8&t=15s&ab_channel=TED.

CHAPTER 2

"BBA Marketing Class Gives Unique Real-World Experience to Students." Emory Business. Accessed on August 31, 2020. https://www.emorybusiness.com/2017/05/22/bba-marketing-class-gives-unique-real-world-experience-to-students/.

CHAPTER 3

"ABA Employment Summary." USC Gould School of Law. Accessed August 31, 2020. https://gould.usc.edu/careers/jd/students/statistics/.

China Heritage: The Wairarapa Academy for New Sinology. "The Best is Like Water." http://chinaheritage.net/journal/the-best-is-like-water/.

"Everything You Need to Know About OCI: On-Campus Interviewing." ABA for Law Students: Before the Bar (BB). Accessed August 31, 2020. https://abaforlawstudents.com/2018/07/01/everything-you-need-to-know-about-oci-on-campus-interviewing/.

"The Phases of OCI: Phase 2 – Preselection & On-Campus Interviews." University of Denver: Sturm College of Law - Career Connection. Accessed September 1, 2020. https://lawcareerblog.law.du.edu/blog/2017/07/26/the-phases-of-oci-phase-2-preselection-on-campus-interviews/.

Wang, Jesse. "The Confucian Christian: A Study on the Rhetorical and Ideological Accommodation of Alfonso Vagnone's Illustrations of the Grand Dao (達道紀言). Emory Theses and Dissertations (ETD) Repository (April 2018): 36-37. https://etd.library.emory.edu/concern/etds/zc77sq117?locale=zh.

"Worry." Association for Behavioral and Cognitive Therapies (ABCT). Accessed August 31, 2020. https://www.abct.org/Information/?m=mInformation&fa=fs_WORRY.

CHAPTER 4

Fessler, Leah. "'You're No Genius': Her Father's Shutdowns Made Angela Duckworth a World Expert on Grit." *Quartz*, March 26, 2018. https://qz.com/work/1233940/angela-duckworth-explains-grit-is-the-key-to-success-and-self-confidence/.

Global Legal Hackathon. "Global Legal Hackathon: World's Largest Legal Hackathon." Accessed September 3, 2020. https://globallegalhackathon.com/.

Rowen, Laurie. "Meet Dorna Moini: Founder of LegalTech Company Documate," Montage Legal Group, April 29, 2019. https://montagelegal.com/meet-dorna-moini-founder-of-legaltech-company-documate/.

Thomas Reuters Legal Executive Institute. "Leveraging Legal Technology to Improve Access to Justice." Accessed September 10, 2020. https://www.legalexecutiveinstitute.com/leveraging-legal-tech-access-to-justice/#:~:text=The%20most%20common%20way%20olegal,online%20for%20attorneys%20and%20individuals.&text=Law%20firm%20attorneys%20can%20use,they're%20onot%20familiar%20with.

CHAPTER 5

"Defend Your Rights. Fight for Change." Juris. Accessed September 3, 2020. https://getjuris.com/.

Sutevski, Dragan. "How to Find the Gap in an Established Market." *Entrepreneurship in a Box* (blog). Accessed September 3, 2020. https://www.entrepreneurshipinabox.com/12388/how-to-find-the-gap-in-an-established-market/.

CHAPTER 6

TED. "The Danger of a Single Story | Chimamanda Ngozi Adichie." October 7, 2009. Video. 19:16. https://www.youtube.com/watch?v=D9Ihs241zeg&t=249s&ab_channel=TED.

CHAPTER 7

"About One Medical." One Medical. Accessed September 10, 2020. https://www.onemedical.com/faq/.

"Infrequently Asked Questions." Fake and Basic. Accessed September 10, 2020. https://fakeandbasic.com/about/

CHAPTER 8

"The Power of Small Wins." *Harvard Business Review.* Accessed September 10, 2020. https://hbr.org/2011/05/the-power-of-small-wins

CHAPTER 9

Boyes, Alice. "Don't Let Perfection Be the Enemy of Productivity." *Harvard Business Review.* March 3, 2020. https://hbr.org/2020/03/dont-let-perfection-be-the-enemy-of-productivity.

Ciobanu, Andrew and Stephen M. Terrell. "Out of the Darkness: Overcoming Depression among Lawyers." *GPSolo*, Vol. 32, No. 2, Health care (Spring 2015): 36-39. https://www-jstor-org.libproxy2.usc.edu/stable/pdf/24632498.pdf?ab_segments=0%-2Fbasic_SYC-5152%2Ftest&refreqid=search%3Ab2daa67c-782e07d99a7de0b1e9f7dc54.

Litt, Joanna. "'Big Law Killed My Husband': An Open Letter from a Sidley Partner's Widow." Law.com: *The American Lawyer*. November 12, 2018. https://www.law.com/americanlawyer/2018/11/12/big-law-killed-my-husband-an-open-letter-from-a-sidley-partners-widow/?slreturn=20200810162318.

Morse, Robert, Ari Castonguay, and Juan Vega-Rodriguez. "Methodology: 2021 Best Law Schools Rankings Find out how U.S. News ranks law schools." *U.S. News & World Report*. March 16, 2020. https://www.usnews.com/education/best-graduate-schools/articles/law-schools-methodology.

Packel, Dan. "Utah Justices Give OK to 'Regulatory Sandbox.'" Law.com: *The American Lawyer*. August 14, 2020. https://www.law.com/americanlawyer/2020/08/14/utah-justices-give-ok-to-regulatory-sandbox/.

CHAPTER 10

Weiss, Debra Cassens. "Did Overwork Kill Skadden Associate? Inconclusive Autopsy Points to Cardiac Issues." *ABA Journal*. November 16, 2011. https://www.abajournal.com/news/article/did_overwork_kill_skadden_associate_inconclusive_autopsy_points_to_cardiac_.

CHAPTER 11

"About Us." Gavelytics. Accessed September 12, 2020. https://www.gavelytics.com/about-us/.

O'Keefe, Kevin. "Rick Merrill, CEO of Gavelytics, on Executing an Idea." Legal Tech Founders. September 17, 2018. https://www.legaltechfounder.com/2018/09/rick-merrill-ceo-gavelytics-executing-idea/.

CHAPTER 12

Maslin, Janet. "FILM REVIEW; Waging a Mythic Battle to Preserve a Pristine Forest." *New York Times.* September 27, 1999. https://www.nytimes.com/1999/09/27/movies/film-review-waging-a-mythic-battle-to-preserve-a-pristine-forest.html.

Princess Mononoke. IMDb. Accessed September 12, 2020. https://www.imdb.com/title/tt0119698/.

CHAPTER 13

Kadohata, Cynthia. *Kira-Kira.* New York: Antheneum Books for Young Readers, 2004.

CHAPTER 14

California Legislative Information. "Assembly Bill No. 1997 CHAPTER 612." Accessed September 13, 2020. https://leginfo.legislature.ca.gov/faces/billNavClient.xhtml?bill_id=201520160AB1997.

County Welfare Directors Association of California. "Commercial Sexual Exploitation of Children (CSEC)." Accessed September 12, 2020. https://www.cwda.org/csec#:~:text=California%20children%20who%20are%20sexually,brought%20into%20the%20child%20welfare.

Hale, Timothy M. and Joseph C. Kvedar. "Privacy and Security Concerns in Telehealth." *AMA Journal of Ethics*, Vol. 2 (2014): 216-221. doi: 10.1001/virtualmentor.2014.16.12.jdsc1-1412.

Tahir, Sabaa. "Katniss Everdeen Is My Hero." *New York Times*, October 18, 2018. https://www.nytimes.com/2018/10/18/books/katniss-everdeen-hunger-games.html.

CHAPTER 15

Benson, Buster. "Live Like a Hydra: Thoughts on how to get stronger when things are chaotic." Medium, August 24, 2013. https://medium.com/better-humans/live-like-a-hydra-c02337782a89.

Taleb, Nassim Nicholas. *The Black Swan: The Impact of the Highly Improbable*. New York: Random House, 2007.

CONCLUSION

Cision: PR Newswire. "University Partnership with Williams College Enrolled Students will have Ongoing, No-Cost Access to Licensed Therapists through Talkspace Online Therapy." Accessed September 15, 2020. https://www.prnewswire.com/news-releases/talkspace-announces-first-university-partnership-with-williams-college-300914660.html.

Duckworth, Angela. "FAQ: What is Grit?" Accessed September 15, 2020. https://angeladuckworth.com/qa/.

Made in the USA
Las Vegas, NV
18 January 2021

16097185R00125